The Complete Chicken

Pam Percy

Endpapers, left:
Poultry from the Exhibitions
The cover of the January 1877 American Agriculturist *reflected the country's fascination with fancy fowls with an engraving of "Poultry from the Exhibitions."*

Endpapers, right:
The New Comers in the Poultry-Yard
This engraving from **an 1874 issue of the American Agriculturalist heralded the arrival of the Crevecoeur in American farmyards. The accompanying article noted that the newly imported French fowls had two-part combs that stand up like horns. The breed "presents such an odd appearance, that we do not wonder that th***e rest of the inhabitants in the barn-yard stare at the strangers."*

Page 1:
A handsome couple
This is an 1890 print of Brown Leghorns from a painting by J. W. Ludlow, one of the world's foremost chicken artists. Due to his meticulous style, his paintings were often used as a standard for the breeds. A dose of Victorian sentimentality is added as the hen gazes at a butterfly.

Page 2:
Contemplating the other side
This handsome rooster is gazing across a distant road, perhaps wondering about life on the other side and contemplating whether or not to cross. (Photograph © Lynn M. Stone)

Page 3:
Weathervane, late 1800s
Weathervanes were invented by the ancient Greeks, who believed that the winds had personalities and possessed prophetic properties. The asymmetry of the shape of the cock allows it to turn in the wind.

Page 6:
"Leading Breeds of Chickens," 1912
The popularity of certain chicken breeds has changed throughout the history of chickens. The favorites in 1912 were all members of the American Standard of Perfection *(see chapter 2) at that time.*

This edition published in 2011 by CRESTLINE
a division of BOOK SALES, INC.
276 Fifth Avenue Suite 206
New York, New York 10001
USA

This edition published by arrangement with Voyageur Press, Inc.
400 First Avenue North, Suite 300, Minneapolis, Minnesota, 55401

Edited by Amy Rost-Holtz
Designed by Maria Friedrich
Printed in Hong Kong

10 9 8 7 6 5 4 3 2 1

Library of Congress Cataloging-in-Publication Data

Percy, Pam, 1949–
The complete chicken : an entertaining history of chickens / Pam Percy.
p. cm.
ISBN-13: 978-0-7858-2754-2
1. Chickens. I. Title.
SF487 .P385 2002
636.5—dc21

2002002627

Dedication

This book is dedicated to Marty, who shares my love of chickens.

Acknowledgments

I would like to thank my friends, who have endured my chicken obsession throughout the years and who have bestowed wonderful chicken gifts upon me, especially Joan, Rita, Laura, Wendy, Karen, Amy, Pam, Eithne, Nate, and my special friend Chappie Fox, of circus fame. Thanks also to those who have helped in my ten years of research, especially Monica Verona, Loyl Stromberg, Barbara Morris, John L. Skinner, Vicki Nelson and the Milwaukee Public Library for the use of their wonderful library archives. I would like to thank my editor Amy Rost-Holtz, who believed in the project when others weren't convinced that there was a world of chicken lovers out there. Most important, I want to thank my family for their enthusiastic support: my mother Thelma who died in 2001 and would have been so proud of the finished product; my father George; my sister Karen; brother Donny; brother-in-law Bill; and my three wonderful children Matt, Katie, and Ross. And a special thanks to my husband Marty Hintz whose love and support was instrumental in making this project finally happen.

"Mode Chantecler"

This vintage postcard depicts the ultimate in chicken headwear.

WHITE & BUFF LEGHORNS
JAPANESE & GAME BANTAMS
BUFF & WHITE WYANDOTTE
BARRED & BUFF PLYMOUTH ROCKS
BLACK MINORCAS
RHODE ISLAND REDS
BLACK & WHITE ORPINGTONS
PARTRIDGE & BUFF COCHINS
LIGHT & DARK BRAHMAS

Contents

Introduction

My name is Pam and I am coming out—out of the coop—and admitting to the world that I am obsessed with chickens. This "problem" began in 1986 when I bought a five-acre farm in River Hills, a town twelve miles north of Milwaukee. The property boasted numerous outbuildings, including several dilapidated chicken coops. My new neighbor, Doug, welcomed me with thirty assorted chickens (a self-serving housewarming gift, since he had grown tired of them). Though I had never consciously laid eyes on a living chicken before, little did I know that I was about to become a full-fledged chicken farmer.

Since I knew nothing about chickens beyond baking and stewing them, I was shocked when total bedlam broke out in the yard. There was abundant bickering, fighting, and downright orneriness. The reason? There were twelve roosters—way too many egos for a peaceful flock. Not having the heart, stomach, or know-how to be the executioner, I sent the surplus roosters to a butcher. I had no desire to eat them. Fresh eggs from the hens were my reward.

Facing page:
Smile for the camera
This chicken poses regally. The color of his beautiful comb and wattles blends in harmoniously with the barn. (Photograph © Alan & Sandy Carey)

Inset:
Chicken courting
This early-1900s postcard portrays a courteous cock who attempts to woo the demure hen—dispelling his reputation of the randy rooster.

Chickens in the kitchen

These are a small portion of my collection of chicken coffee cups and other chickenalia, including a taxidermy chicken comfortably nestled on plastic eggs. (Photograph by Ricky Heldt)

Life on the chicken farm became tranquil for a while. The hens were laying. There was no squabbling. The brood was semi-free range, which means they roamed by day but were locked up at night. Although keeping an accurate head count was difficult because they hardly ever stood still, I eventually noticed that the brood was dwindling. I then began to find the carcasses of my precious pets. The culprits? Raccoons. I began an endless battle to fend off the varmints by fixing walls and building new safety areas.

My flock has varied in size throughout the years. Now I have a small company called Pampered Poultry through which I raise and sell free-range chickens and eggs.

During my many years as a chicken enthusiast, some of the birds earned special places in my heart. Although naming them was not my habit, occasionally a moniker was too perfect to resist. For example, "Thunder Thighs" was a sweet, maternal buff Cochin with bulbous legs and a healthy appetite. One pompous rooster, who we referred to as that "Old Fool," disliked men and attacked any males who dared to enter what he considered his personal space. My favorite was the "car chicken," because every time I opened the car door, she tried to get in. She greeted me when I got home from work, loved to be petted, and ate from my hand. I even let her sleep in the front hall closet when it was too cold outside. I secretly think she just wanted to be with me.

I am often asked, "Why chickens?"

To me, chickens are beautiful creatures and relaxing to watch. I love looking out my window and seeing them bustle around in the yard. They have an interesting social structure and, contrary to popular opinion, are quite smart. They are constantly busy, a state to which I can easily relate.

Perhaps my admiration of chickens is a throwback to my English heritage, because the British have long been great fowl fanciers. Maybe it is genetic, because my father raised Rhode Island Reds as a boy near Boston. Or possibly it is my desire not to be totally overtaken by a modern, prepackaged culture. In my mind, chickens have a timeless quality about them. They create a gentle pace.

Whatever the reason, I love chickens.

Once the word got out that I was raising chickens, my friends bestowed upon me various sorts of chicken things. Soon my house filled with beautiful "chickenalia." I also began sneaking off to antique and collectible shops, in search of elusive chicken treasure. My collection of "objects de chicken" began to grow . . . and grow . . . and grow. . . .

The Complete Chicken project began when I visited the Milwaukee Public Library a number of years ago, and I realized that no one had compiled a coffee-table book on chickens in art, culture, and history. I was indignant that the chicken had been so overlooked. I am constantly amazed that—other than for scientific data and chicken cuisine—very little has been written about these wonderful birds. I decided to rectify that situation.

Resigning from my job as the managing director of a theater company in Milwaukee, I set out to discover the world of chickens in art, culture, history, and many other areas. For almost a year, I scoured the

A cozy corner of the dining room

Our dining room has become my chicken sanctuary. The wall proudly displays an antique appliqued chicken weathervane, a Jimmy Lee Sudduth chicken painting (see chapter 3), and a Blue Ridge chicken plate. On the chest of drawers are hand-carved folk chickens, including one of my favorites: a humorous woodcarving of a hen contemplating her egg. I refer to the statue on the left, by Todd Warner, as my "Giacometti chicken," after the artist known for his elongated human sculptures. (Photograph by Ricky Heldt)

Life With the Birds

Although the personalities of individual birds vary greatly and generalization is dangerous, certain assertions can be made with regard to chickens. The hen and rooster are not only a dysfunctional couple, they also typify the outmoded stereotype of the male/female relationship. In other words, the old perception of male supremacy and female submission is reality in the chicken world.

Roosters, in general, are proud, arrogant, and promiscuous as they strut and rut around the yard, often terrorizing the hens (and humans, for that matter). On the other hand, hens are the picture of stoic domesticity and the supreme symbol of motherhood as they patiently and stubbornly sit on their eggs. At other times, hens keep busy doing stereotypically feminine activities, such as bustling around the yard with their brood of chicks, preening, and luxuriously wallowing in dust baths.

Although hens are usually quite docile and sweet, I've seen them be very mean-spirited toward other chickens—especially to those on the lower end of the pecking order.

Milwaukee Public Library, the Golda Meir Library at the University of Wisconsin–Milwaukee, and libraries in Madison, Chicago, New York, and even London. The Smithsonian Institution is a repository of great chicken art, as are the National Gallery, The Abby Aldrich Rockefeller Folk Art Museum in Colonial Williamsburg, and other art museums throughout the country.

Knowing only that Picasso and Manet had included chickens in a few of their paintings, I embarked on a journey toward chicken enlightenment. Unaware of what lurked on the shelves, I could barely contain my joy upon each "chicken find."

I was obsessed. I barely slept. My adrenaline soared as I entered each facility, eager and ready for the hunt. I spent hours and days in search of the next "chicken find."

I developed a talent for "fanning" books and spotting chickens on their pages. I developed a "chicken seventh sense" when I walked into an antique shop.

It was crazy.

I was crazed.

I dreamed about chickens. All I could talk about was chickens. I began to bore even myself.

The result of this search was profound and my learning curve overwhelming. I was delighted to discover that, throughout history in various cultures, the chicken has often been a symbol—one that has been worshiped, adored, abhorred, sacrificed, maligned, ridiculed, sentimentalized, and idealized. Artists have reflected upon this diversity in paintings, sculptures, illustrations, and cartoons. The chicken has been featured in literature, advertising, music, political rhetoric, movies, and many other creative outlets.

People have wildly varied reactions when I say I have written a book about chickens. Listeners usually fall into one of two camps. They are either chicken cynics, snickering or making sarcastic quips about chickens, or they are chicken champions and respond enthusiastically. Chicken cynicism probably stems from an age-old attitude that focuses too much on the chicken's sometimes negative qualities. Derogatory connotations regarding the word *chicken* usually begin in childhood with the obnoxious refrain, "So-and-so is a chicken." Later on, the person who may have ridiculed others could become a "cocky so-and-so." Even later, there is the possibility of becoming a "henpecked" old fool.

I hope that this book will elevate these cynical, low opinions of the chicken. It aims to create a chicken awareness with a final goal of chicken enlightenment. Once you have developed a chicken consciousness, you begin to realize that chickens are *everywhere*. After reading this book, you will not only have a clear vision of the "Complete Chicken," but you will come to the startling realization that the history of the chicken reflects the history of the world.

In 2002, Americans will eat an average of 81 pounds of chicken, compared with 60 pounds of beef and 52 pounds of pork.

It is a common misconception that the word *chicken* refers to the female of the species. In fact, *chicken* refers to both the hen and the rooster.

Chicken taxi

This chicken art comes from an early twentieth-century promotional calendar from the Hayes Litho Company of Buffalo, New York.

Chapter 1

Chicken History: Which, When, and Where

The question "Which came first—the chicken or the egg?" has baffled humans for eons. Now the butt of many a joke, this popular conundrum was mused over by such philosophers as Aristotle (384–322 B.C.) and Plutarch (c. A.D. 46–120). Although it was later dismissed as a trite intellectual exercise by Ulisse Aldrovandi, the Renaissance chicken expert, reputations were once staked on this vital issue. The early Christian church insisted that all living creatures were created by God and opposed those who believed that life evolves from seeds, or eggs, in the case of our present-day plumpers. But I don't wish to dwell on the profundity of evolution. Sometimes the question is more interesting than the answer.

There also has been much speculation about *when* the chicken first appeared on the earth. According to Charles Darwin, the Grandfather of Evolution, the predecessor to the first real chicken (known as *Gallus gallus* in Latin) was a Red Jungle Fowl. It is now generally believed that this pre-chicken was domesticated in the sprawling forests of southern and southwestern Asia sometime around 10,000 B.C. The Red Jungle Fowl's original habitat included all of India up the rugged Himalayan foothills, as well as today's nations of Myanmar (Burma), Malaysia, and Thailand. This self-sufficient fowl could fly like a pheasant and was able to fend for itself with its strong beak and sharp talons; its chicks were also self reliant, able to scurry around and feed on insects soon after hatching.

Facing page:
Welcome to the world
After twenty-one days of incubation, either by a mother hen sitting on her eggs or an incubator, the chick pecks out of its egg. Immediately, it is eager to scratch, peck, and pick for food. A chick can last thirty-six hours without water, which makes shipping day-old chickens possible. (Photograph © Lynn M. Stone)

Inset:
Chicken stamps
This 1948 stamp celebrated the centennial of the U.S. Poultry Industry. It is just one of the approximately 500 stamps from all over the world that bear the image of a chicken. In a 1949 Life *magazine article, the journalist expressed indignation over the choice of this stamp by the U.S. Postal Service. Obviously, the author was not chicken enlightened.*

Our "first" chicken

This depiction of "Jungle Fowl" was rendered by C. H. Weigall for the Illustrated Book of Domestic Poultry *(1854), edited by Martin Doyle. The jungle fowl on the left is a Red Jungle Fowl. The Sonnerat's on the right is not related to the domestic fowl.*

Other scientists theorize that chickens and their ancestors popped up simultaneously in other locations around the world. Supporting this idea is the existence of the Araucana, a unique breed that lays blue-green eggs and developed in an isolated region in South America. When the Spaniards invaded Mexico in the 1500s, chickens had already been established in the Incan culture.

It is generally believed that *Gallus gallus* became *Gallus domesticus* sometime between 3200 and 2000 B.C. Surprisingly, chickens were not captured and tamed to feed humankind. Instead, they were originally domesticated for their fighting ability—hence the first-known spectator blood sport, cockfighting. Cockfighting was more than simple entertainment and an opportunity for gambling; it served as an alternative to battle when rivals met in a dispute.

People also found the plucky poultry to be excellent timekeepers, greeting the dawn with their raucous wake-up calls. The birds were a type of primitive household security system with their cawing and cackling when alarmed. As the ancient Malaysians migrated along the great river gorges of Asia, they kept cocks close at hand. On these perilous journeys, the birds' crowing warned of danger and counted off the days, even in the murky recesses of the dense jungle.

A beautiful rooster was a cherished possession to these long-ago people in Southeast Asia. They felt there was a mystique about chickens; the birds' aloof behavior radiated wisdom and beatific serenity. Such an animal was seen as blessed by the gods, and the fowl became sacred in many cultures. Chickens were regularly offered to various deities as a substitute for human sacrifice and to ward off evil.

The Archaeopteryx, a carnivore that stood on two legs and had wings and feathers, is thought to have roamed the earth with the dinosaurs 150 million years ago. The Archaeopteryx is believed to be the predecessor of today's birds, including the chicken.

There is speculation that the chicken received its Latin name, *Gallus,* from the strange Galli priests, who were said to have drunk from the River Gallus, which caused madness. Their mysterious religion was one of the early rivals of Christianity, and the Christian apologists used the Galli as an example of everything abhorrent about pagan cultures. The Gallis were reported to have ritualistic orgies complete with self-mutilation, castration, and the drinking and smearing of blood. They were dedicated to the goddess Cybele, and the rooster was associated with Attis, Cybele's male, human partner.

Clay sculptures of abstract chickens dating to 2000 B.C. have been found near the Yellow and Yangtze Rivers of China.

Facing page:
"This is Plato's man"
The classical thinking of Plato and Diogenes was humorously rendered around 1525 in Diogenes *by Ugo da Carpi, a painter and printmaker, who is credited as the first Italian to use the technique of chiaroscuro woodcuts (a technique in which several wood blocks are used to create one print, giving the woodcut various tones). This important piece portrays a man shadowed by the satirical image of a rooster that is not only defeathered but also has its head screwed on backward. (Ugo da Carpi,* Diogenes, *Pepita Milmore Memorial Fund, photograph © Board of Trustees, National Gallery of Art, Washington, D.C.)*

From Southeast Asia, the chicken migrated both west and east. Slowly, it made its way through the Middle East and north to Europe, as well as moving toward China and then Japan. When India conquered Persia (now Iran) in the fourth century B.C., the Persians passed on their avid interest in chickens and cockfighting. When the chicken arrived in Greece, the Greeks referred to it as the Persian Bird. The rooster was sacred to Mithras, the Persian sun god. In the ancient Persian religion called Zoroastrianism (Zarathustra), the cock and the dog were sacred and protectors against evil. Devout Zoroastrians had a cock to fend off evil spirits with his boisterous cry. A white rooster was viewed as an angel, one who blocked Satan's nefarious schemes. A verse by the Persian poet Chanakya, written about 300 B.C., claimed there are four things to be learned from a cock: to fight, to get up early, to eat with your family, and to protect your wife when she gets into trouble. (Ah, maybe that should be wives—roosters are very polygamous!)

Egyptian Chickens

The chicken became an integral part of Egyptian life sometime in the first or second century A.D., although there is earlier evidence that chickens existed there before the time of Christ. As early as the fifteenth century B.C., the Annals of Thutmose III, one of Egypt's pharaohs, describe birds that "bear every day," presumably chickens, brought back from Babylonia. Researchers have described an icon of a chick found in the tomb of Tutankhamen (c. 1400 B.C.), and there is a cock in a scene depicted in the tomb of Rekhmara (c. 1500 B.C.) at Thebes. Egyptian king Ikhnaton (c. 1372–1354 B.C.) refers to the chicken in "Hymn to the Sun."

In Egypt, as opposed to Greece and Rome in later years, the role of the chicken appeared to be utilitarian rather than a spiritual one. As early as the fourth century B.C., the Egyptians started to mass produce chickens and incubate eggs, presumably to feed the throng of pyramid workers. They created the process of incubation in "hatching ovens" and were capable of producing from 15 to 20 million chicks a season. The Egyptians also made great advances in animal husbandry and the development of breeds for eggs and meat.

Greek Chickens

In ancient Greece, the birthplace of Western thought, the chicken was transformed into a creature with a higher purpose. It became the subject of intellectual thought, literary reference, scientific scrutiny, and numerous myths and legends. The cock was considered a creature of tremendous beauty and strength and was associated with numerous Greek gods. Cockfighting was popular, and the rooster became a symbol of masculinity, virility, bravery, and fertility.

Many Greek thinkers reflected on the significance of the chicken. Plato (c. 428–347 B.C.) once described man as merely a "featherless biped." Diogenes (c. 320 B.C.), a philosopher from the Cynic school of Greek thought, replied by plucking a fowl and taking it to Plato's lecture, claiming that it was "Plato's man."

The Lex Salica, a collection of laws created under the reign of French king Clovis I (A.D. 466?–511), mention the punishment for stealing poultry.

A boy with large cock
This interesting fifth century B.C. terra-cotta statue of a naked young boy sporting a cock-like hat, seated next to a very large cock with similar headdress reflects the symbolic nature of the cock during this period. Throughout history, the cock has often had a sexual connotation. (All rights reserved, The Metropolitan Museum of Art, Rogers Fund, 1906. [06.1087])

Socrates (470?–399 B.C.), Plato's friend and teacher, made a noteworthy chicken reference on his deathbed. It was then a common practice to sacrifice a cock to Aesculapius, the god of health, in hopes of eternal life, to ward off sickness, or as a thank-you for recovery. At age seventy, Socrates was sentenced to death by the ingestion of hemlock. As the poison was taking effect, Socrates last words were to his friend Crite, "We owe a cock to Aesculapius. Pay it and do not neglect it."

The philosopher Aristotle was prolific on the subject of chickens, and some of his observations were undisputed for many years. In addition to offering his theory on "the chicken and the egg," he was the first to study the embryonic development of the chicken, opening and accurately describing the contents of eggs during each day of their incubation. Some of his scientific offerings are less credible. He suggested that chickens suffering from eye problems should be treated by smearing their eyes with a mixture of mother's milk, cumin, honey, and other ingredients, then led into the shade. For chickens with diarrhea, he suggested feeding the birds a pulverized mash of meal and onion in wine.

In Greek mythology, the chicken was sacred to Athena, who was the goddess of wisdom and warfare, the patron of the city of Athens, and the "trumpeter of justice." Athena also happened to have the cock's bellicose nature. Demeter, the goddess of agriculture, and her daughter Persephone claimed the chicken as a symbol of fertility and the rising spring, while Hermes, the god of commerce and a busy, productive polygamist, possessed the cock's erotic attributes. The cock's crowing at dawn caused him to be connected with gods of creation and to Helios, the Greek sun god. His reputation as a lover put him in alliance with Eros, the god of love and desire.

According to Aelian, a Greek author in the second century, Hercules and his wife Hebe kept hens at the Temple of Hebe and cocks in the Temple of Hercules. "The males, stimulated with lust, they flew across the river and after they had impregnated the females, they returned to their god and to their purified dwelling, purged by the river that ran between by which each sex was divided." This certainly is a myth, because the randy rooster is always lusty, often servicing dozens of hens per day. If the tale were true, this would constitute a lot of river jumping.

Myths aside, chickens were an important part of daily life in Greece. The playwright Aristophanes (c. 448–385 B.C.) said that even the poorest Athenian kept a hen for laying eggs. Depictions of chickens on Greek sarcophagi portrayed cocks being fed, carried, and stroked. Pet cocks were buried with elaborate tombstones. "Nourish a cock, but sacrifice it not" was a common Greek saying, for cocks were sacred either to the sun or moon. Pythagoras (fl. 530 B.C.), the brilliant mathematician, scientist, philosopher, and preacher of mystic doctrines, warned that a white cock in particular should never be sacrificed, because it was sacred to the moon.

In Greece, the cock was associated with homosexual affairs and was often a love-gift from an older man to a young boy he wished to seduce. A well-known terra-cotta statue in the Olympia Archaeological Museum portrays Zeus holding Ganymede, who is in turn holding a cock, an icon of male erotic urge. Beginning in Greece and continuing into the Roman Empire, the cock was an important symbol of the sexual prowess of a man.

Etruscan Chickens

The ancient Etruscans, highly cultured residents of the Italian peninsula, also made chickens an important part of their culture before they succumbed to Roman rule in the sixth century B.C. Soothsayers used the "hen oracle" to foretell the future through alectromancy—a divination process where hens answered life's most pressing problems by eating corn. A high priest interpreted the order in which they pecked at the kernels as an indication of the future.

The Etruscans also originated the "wishbone" custom, where two people make secret wishes while each pulling on one end of a dried chicken clavicle bone. Supposedly, the wish is granted to whomever gets the largest piece. This practice was later adapted by the English and transported to America. When the Pilgrims celebrated a feast of Thanksgiving at Plymouth in 1621, turkey bones would have been their clavicle of choice—turkeys being more plentiful than chickens in the New World.

Roman Chickens

The fortune of the Roman chickens paralleled the rise and fall of the Roman Empire. At the empire's pinnacle, the chicken was a central figure in the period's religious rituals and was considered sacred, with numerous magical properties. The bird was valued for its supposed medicinal powers and as an important food source. During this time, great advances were made in poultry science by Roman farmers and in gastronomy by Roman chefs. As in earlier cultures, cockfighting remained an integral part of the Roman world. Soldiers used cocks as "watchmen," tying a bird to a chariot so an alarm would be raised if someone tried to steal the cart.

The Romans continued the Etruscan belief that the chicken had divine powers and could communicate with the netherworld. The cock was the preferred medium of those Roman alectromancers; along with wishbones, stones (called alectorii) found in the stomach of cocks supposedly had the same wish-giving properties if read correctly by a priest. Priests cut up sacrificed chickens and "read" the entrails to foretell the future, a process called haruspicy. In another divination process called *oraculum ex tripudio,* military decisions were based solely on a chicken's appetite. If the chicken ate, there would be a victory. A famous story is told of the battle of Drepana during the Punic Wars in 249 B.C. Chickens were brought to the flagship to determine if there should be a battle. The birds, possibly with a case of seasickness, declined supper. The consul, P. Claudius Pulcher, became furious and threw the poor chickens overboard, roaring, "If they won't eat, let them drink!" The Romans lost that battle.

During the Roman period, the chicken was closely scrutinized by great philosophers such as Columella (first century A.D.), who liberally wrote about agricultural subjects. Varro (c. 116–29 B.C.), the "father" of Roman natural history, and Pliny the Elder (A.D. 23–79), a natural history author, also carefully studied the world of fowl. Their observations of the birds, detailed research, and thoughtful writing greatly advanced the subject of poultry science. Both Varro and Columella discussed the various breeds of chickens and remarked on big profits to be

Greek vase with Ganymede and cock

This is one of the many examples of Greek vases portraying the image of a chicken. It is attributed to the Pan Painter (c. 480–460 B.C.). Here, Ganymede, the young boy who was the object of Zeus' desire, is fleeing with cock in hand. Cocks were often gifts from older Greek men to young boys they wished to seduce. (All rights reserved, The Metropolitan Museum of Art, Rogers Fund, 1923. [23.160.55])

In the King James Bible, Job 38:36 usually reads, "Who hath put wisdom in the inward parts? or who hath given understanding to the heart?" But some scholars suggest it can also be translated as, "Who hath put wisdom in the ibis, or who hath given understanding to the cock?"

Cockfighting

One day, a seemingly sweet man named Dang arrived on my doorstep. He was Hmong, part of the large population of Southeast Asians who had moved to Milwaukee after supporting the American cause in the Vietnam War. Dang had noticed my chickens and my coops, and he kindly offered to fix them and help me around the farm in exchange for letting him use the buildings to raise his own chickens. The offer sounded too good to be true, and I immediately agreed.

The Cock Pit
This engraving by William Hogarth, portrays one element of the cockfighting world in British society. From lowlife to royalty, the sport permeated all classes, and reached its peak of popularity in England before it was banned by Queen Victoria in 1849.

It wasn't long before Dang and his many friends created an amazing labyrinth of chicken cages in my outbuildings. Although I wasn't crazy about the fact that my driveway looked like a used car lot when they arrived in droves to care for their birds, practicality won over. After all, I was getting new chicken coops. However, I noticed that his gangly chickens were rather strangely shaped compared to my own plump, calm fowl in adjoining pens. Dang's dozens of birds had a reform school look about them, rather like a Far Side cartoon come to life. They had feisty dispositions and the gimlet eyes of villains seen only in bad Italian-made Westerns. They sported disproportionately long legs, they were unspectacular in coloring, and they were *big*. Yet beyond thinking they were ugly, I didn't pay much attention.

Then, on a hen-purchasing hunt, I visited another farmer who showed me a chicken that looked like Dang's. He mentioned that I probably wouldn't be interested in that bird because it was a fighting cock. I immediately envisioned swarms of snarling police and SPCA inspectors swooping down on my quiet little farmsite, with the resulting headlines in our local newspapers blaring, "River Hills Maven in Legal Stew as Mastermind Behind Fighting Cock Scandal."

I knew cockfighting was illegal in Wisconsin, but I wasn't sure if inadvertently allowing what might be nascent fighting cocks to be raised on one's property was also against the law. Even though he did not seem to be doing anything illegal on the surface, I decided that Dang and his cocks had to go. I didn't want to involve the authorities, so I tried on my own to convince Dang and his friends to depart. They eventually did—begrudgingly—with their cackling, kickboxing critters under their arms.

Cockfighting claims to be the oldest spectator sport in the world. Cocks were domesticated and bred for fighting long before the chicken was considered a gourmet delight. History tells us that cockfighting probably began in India. It spread east to China and west to Greece and Rome, and from there to Great Britain, other parts of Western Europe, and on to America.

The fighting cock symbolized unyielding courage and a willingness to die rather than lead a life of servitude. Ion of Chios (c. 490 B.C.), a poet, dramatist, and philosopher said of the dying cock, "He falls to earth not yet crushed in body or both eyes by the blows, but with failing strength he groans and refuses to live a slave." Though cockfighting was introduced to the Greeks long before, Themistocles (c. 527–462 B.C.) made it a national sport and organized yearly cockfights in Athens to inspire his troops. In Greece and Rome, cockfighting was an important part of daily life. The great thinkers and writers of the day wrote extensively on the subject. Pliny the Elder described the cock's lust for fighting even to death and claimed their sovereignty absolute, even ascribing to them the power to terrorize the lion and basilisk. Columella (first century A.D.) described professional cock trainers who lost all their outlay on their birds in gambling. Plutarch (c. A.D. 46–120) criticized the rich for indulging in cockfighting and derided Caesar's cocks for losing. Much was written about which cocks to breed, how to train and feed them, and their valor and prizes.

Early Christians throughout Europe portrayed cockfights on columns on numerous churches, the images positioned prominently in scenes from the Old Testament, the Holy Family's Flight to Egypt, and the lives of Christ and the saints. Cockfighting was depicted on gravestones and funerary altars to symbolize the struggle against temptation. The early Christian marriage sarcophagi expressed the idea of conjugal love with portraits of the married couple. Often the pictures depict a cockfight at their feet. I find this somewhat amusing. A cockfight seems a rather negative symbol for marital bliss. However, a more learned scholar explained, "The conjoined cockfight and marriage references evoke another allegory, the Eros-Anteros iconographic cycle, well known in Classical art, in which Cupid and his twin or partner engage in a friendly rivalry representing love and counter-love and also symbolizing matrimony."

From Rome, cockfighting spread north through Italy to Germany, Spain, and throughout England, Wales, and Scotland. In England, cockfighting reached its pinnacle in the Western world as a sport, science, and amusement. Number One Downing Street once housed a cockpit, originally erected by King Henry VIII, an avid cocker. Another of his many royal cockpits in and around London was at Whitehall.

In 1849, under Queen Victoria's directive, cockfighting was finally forbidden in England by the Church of England and by law. One curious exception was a custom that allowed cockfighting on Shrove Tuesday, the day before Lent begins. Young boys would bring their favorite game cock to their master and would partake in cockfighting throughout the day. The pupil whose cock survived was spared from punishment during Lent, and the master received the spoils of the day: all the dead cocks.

Cockfighting also flourished in America. When the settlers arrived, they brought with them chickens and game birds. Even though the Puritans frowned upon cockfighting, it was one of the most popular forms of entertainment throughout the colonies. It was banned in Massachusetts as early as 1836.

In America, all classes of society indulged in cockfighting, a "democratic sport" where wealth and social standing were irrelevant. George Washington was an ardent cocker and subscribed to English cockfighting magazines. Benjamin Franklin attended and refereed cockfights. President Andrew Jackson kept fighting cocks in the White House stables, and other notables, including Henry Clay, John C. Calhoun, and Martin Van Buren also indulged in the sport. In the South, cockfighting was associated with taverns. Often both master and slave shared a common delight in fighting cocks. Allegedly, Honest Abe Lincoln received his nickname due to his fairness in judging cockfights.

Today, cockfighting exists throughout the world, either legally or illegally. It prevails in Mexico, the Philippines, Puerto Rico, Ireland, Columbia, Haiti, the Dominican Republic, Cuba, Jamaica, and elsewhere. Although it is legal only in Louisiana, New Mexico, and Oklahoma, cocks are fought in every state in America, and the sport continues to be part of the gambling culture, an alternative to the mechanized slot machine world. In Virginia, cockfighting is legal if gambling is not involved.

Though banned in Indonesia in 1981, cockfighting is allowed in that country for important Balinese Hindu ceremonies. In the Philippines, cockfighting existed long before Spain colonized the country and legalized the sport for taxes. Today, it is an important part of the Philippine culture. For example, on the Island of Cebu, there is a cockpit in each town, and there are even more in the cities. In Sumatra, fighting cocks were worshipped. A great display of pomp and circumstance surrounded a cockfight. Even the slain bird was honored by being bathed in gums and spices before being cremated, with its ashes placed in a golden pot where they could be revered forever.

The Old Testament refers to Solomon's "fatted fowl," which were most likely chickens. In New Testament times, the crowing of cocks was a familiar sound above the hubbub of Jerusalem's crowded streets and markets.

The noble rooster

In European heraldry, the rooster represents both soldierly courage and religious aspiration.

made by poultry farmers on the island of Delos. They described in detail all the aspects of poultry breeding, keeping, feeding and fattening, and poultry houses (gallinaria).

Myths around the chicken intensified well beyond the dinner table. The cock became identified with numerous gods: His sexiness and lust were personified through Amor (Cupid), the god of love, and associated with Priapus, the god of fertility. His abundance of hens affiliated him with Mercury, the god of property and prosperity, who was also a trickster often resorting to thievery and gambling. The cock's combativeness and willingness to die fighting were perfect matches with Mars and Ares, fierce gods of war.

Just as it was in Greece, in Rome the cock was symbolic of the male erotic urge, homosexual or heterosexual. The cock's sexual prowess was legendary. It was felt that his crow was due to his constant lust and belligerence. The cock is seen in many erotic scenes in art, including an engraved gemstone where the cock is portrayed mounting the hen.

In the court of Caligula (A.D. 12–41), slave girls were summoned for the "dance du poulet" where they entertained that ultimate pervert by attempting to attract the chickens by whatever means they could. The girl who attracted the fewest was smeared with chicken fat and thrown into the royal kennel.

Animal abuse, including that of chickens, became brutal spectacle in the Roman amphitheaters. In one horrendous spectacle called the "Tournament of Beasts," 5,000 animals of all kinds were butchered in a single day. Even children partook in "chicken baiting"—a cruel game in which a chicken was tied by one foot to a pole. The "baiter" sprinkled corn on the ground, and when the chicken began to peck, the baiter would crush its head with a mallet.

European Chickens

Chickens made their mark in Europe after the fall of the Roman Empire, during the period from about A.D. 500 to 1500. Christianity eventually became the dominant religion of the "civilized world," offering a source of spiritual stability for the devout. The early Christians honored the cock as a symbol of Christ; it was felt that the cock's crowing was like the voice of Christ signaling the coming of a new day. It also symbolized the spiritual awakening for those who converted to Christianity. A representation of the rooster was often placed on the top of a church column, tower, or steeple as a symbol of vigilance and as a protector of the landscape.

St. Ambrose, a fourth-century monk who popularized the singing of hymns in church, celebrated this symbolism in the words to his famous choral arrangement, "Ad Galli Cantum":

> Let us rise up valiantly
> The cock rings forth his cry.
> He doth upbraid the slumberers,
> Refutes those who deny.
> When crows the cock,
> Our hope returns,
> Health o'er the sick is poured.
> The robber's sword is safely sheathed,
> The faint find faith restored.

In the Middle Ages, animal allegories known as bestiaries became extremely popular as teaching tools. Second only to the Bible as the prime source of inspiration, they were serious works based on natural history, but also infused with religion, mythology, and science. Bestiaries ranged from sacred to secular, and the status of chickens varied from work to work.

In a French bestiary, written by Hugh de Fouilloy in the mid 1100s, the cock is portrayed as an intelligent and revered creature. De Fouilloy claimed the cock's intelligence was granted directly from heaven, which made it the teacher of truth. The gifted cock's crow wakes up and inspires the preacher. According to de Fouilloy, a preacher even sounds like a rooster when exhorting his parishioners.

But, like all "superior" beings, cocks did not always live up to their potential. De Fouilloy described these birds as being content with themselves, even prone to idleness and the pursuit of pleasures of the flesh. Others failed to wake up the priests and squandered the wisdom God gave them to acquire transitory things. In other words, they were similar to humans.

While many, like de Fouilloy, thought the chicken was admirable, others maligned the poor fowl by inaccurately depicting it as the basilisk (or cockatrice)—reputed to be the most evil of all creatures. Hatched from a cock's egg, the basilisk supposedly had the power to kill with either a glance or its incredibly bad breath. It had existed in myth since the fifth century and was originally depicted as a serpent. By the mid-thirteenth century, it came to be described as a cock with a dragon's or serpent's tail.

The 1218 bestiary of Pierre de Beauvais says, "When the cock is seven years old, to its amazement an egg is formed within it. After great suffering, it secretly seeks a warm place—a dung heap or a stable—where it digs a hole. Three times a day, it goes there in hope of delivery. The toad smells the venom inside the egg and watches carefully

The Talmud says, "Praised be Thou, O God, Lord of the world, that gavest understanding to the cock to distinguish between day and night."

The evil basilisk

The basilisk (or cockatrice) existed in myth beginning in the fifth century. Reputed to be the most evil of all creatures, this half-cock, half-serpent could kill with a glance or by its bad breath. There are stories of soldiers wearing mirrors as armor, presumably because a basilisk could be harmed by seeing its own image.

Chickens in alchemy

In alchemy, chickens were used as archetypal symbols of man and woman. In this 1600s epigram from Michael Maier's Atalanta Fugiens, *the man (cock) represents the sun and the woman (hen) represents the moon.*

"The right testicle of a rooster bound with the skin of a ram" is a potent aphrodisiac, according to Pliny the Elder, although what was to be done with this contrivance is uncertain.

because it wants to hatch the egg. This it does, and when the animal is born it has the upper parts of a cock and the lower body of a snake."

Real animals and mythical beasts, including chickens, were woven into the obscure mystical writings of achemists. Alchemy is an ancient science that combines magic, astrology, science or pseudoscience, mystical philosophy, and the occult. In essence, it strives to unlock the mysterious workings of the universe, to transform metals into gold, and to find the Philosopher's Stone, an elixir of life that would cure disease and lengthen life. Alchemy is extremely complicated and difficult to comprehend due to the clandestine nature of its findings. In alchemy, symbolism is a convenient way to remember things and keep knowledge secret. The union of opposites was an all-important concept to the alchemists, and the rooster and hen were a co-dependent couple. The philosophical cock symbolized the Sun (Sol) and the philosophical hen, on the other hand, represented the Moon (Luna).

Michael Maier (1568–1622) was a prolific writer on various subjects including alchemy. In *Atalanta Fugiens: Sources of an Alchemical Book of Emblems*, Maier focuses on the chicken in Emblem XXX. The motto for that emblem says, "The sun needs the moon, like the cock needs the hen." The corresponding epigram says:

O, Sun, you do not achieve anything alone, if I am not present with my forces,
Just as the cock is useless without the help of the hen.
And in my turn I, the Moon, want your help,
Just as the cock is desired by the hen.
Foolish is he who would want to free from the bonds those things
From which Nature urgently requires that they are united.

The alchemists believed that a cock's egg, if they could find one, was more valuable for magical uses than any other item. In fact, some sorcerers preferred to possess a cock's egg rather than a Philosopher's Stone. Out of the cock's egg, it was believed that the devil could hatch creatures that were "most injurious to all of the Christian faith and race."

As might be expected, the fathers of the Christian church frowned upon the science of alchemy. In 1474, at Basel, Switzerland, legal proceedings were actually taken against an unfortunate cock for allegedly having laid an egg. The accused was labeled a basilisk and charged with being in cahoots with Satan. Although the defense claimed that laying an egg was an involuntary act, the prosecutors retorted that even if the accused was an involuntary agent of the devil, that was a crime unto itself. The cock was convicted and condemned to death—burned at the stake along with his egg.

By the late Middle Ages, there are few references to the cock as a religious figure, most likely due to his sexual prowess and promiscuity. Early church leaders did not want to dredge up any erotic associations having to do with Christ, and the result was the rooster's dramatic fall from grace.

During the Italian Renaissance, the chicken again came under scientific scrutiny. Italian naturalist Ulisse Aldrovandi (c. 1522–1605), who was considered the grandfather of "Chicken Wisdom," wrote a nine-volume treatise on animals, one of which was devoted entirely to chickens. The book contained more than four hundred pages of every conceivable subject relating to chickens. There was some fact and more fiction, but the book provides a fascinating look at the entire body of chicken knowledge in the sixteenth century. Aldrovandi was impressed by the history, physiology, legends, myths, and religious associations of chickens. He described how to raise and cook chickens, including capons. He was charmed by the cock's beauty, bravery, and virility, as well as his reliability as an alarm clock and his fatherly concern for his "wives" and chicks.

Most interesting, however, is Aldrovandi's apothecary. He admired the chicken's many benefits to humans—to Aldrovandi, chickens were veritable medicine cabinets. "They furnish food for both humans who are well and those who are ill and rally those who are almost dead," he wrote. "There is almost no illness of the body, both internal and external, which does not draw its remedy from these birds." Every discomfort and disease known to humankind found relief—we are told—with the chicken. From leprosy to pleurisy, from tumors to humors, from elephantiasis to phlebitis, roosters, hens, or parts thereof were prescribed.

Rooster broth was recommended for flatulence, arthritis, chronic fever, trembling limbs, headaches, nausea, indigestion, asthma, constipation, and even as a deterrent against ferocious panthers and lions. Rooster brains were recommended for alleviating cerebral palsy and as an antidote for the bite of a poisonous animal. Rooster dung was effectively used to induce vomiting.

Rooster testicles served a multitude of remedies. For epilepsy, it was recommended, "Give the fasting patient, the testicles of a rooster ground up in water to drink. Let the patient abstain from wine for ten days. Then dry testicles must be administered and eaten daily as long as necessary." For bed-wetting, eating one testicle was a prescribed cure. The list goes on and on, encouraging us to give thanks for modern medicine.

British Chickens

Prior to Julius Caeser's first invasion of England in 55 B.C., the chicken there merely functioned as a feisty cockfighter. The gourmet delights of the chicken had not yet been discovered by the Brits. Over the ensuing generations, as the Roman hold spread a semblance of tranquillity over the island, selective breeding took hold. Birds were raised for their egg production and meat, as well as an ability to adapt to the island's multi-seasonal climate. Between the 1500s and 1700s, distinct types of chickens were documented, including Hamburgs, Scots Greys, and Dorkings.

In the mid-nineteenth century, the British poultry industry was turned upside down by the arrival of exotic new Chinese breeds. In 1843, the British government forced open Chinese ports to commerce after a long period of hostility and isolation. Among the exotic items imported from the once Secret Kingdom were Shanghais, Cochins, and Brahmas. Cochin cocks were reported to weigh up to fifteen pounds, and the British marveled at the fur-like feathers that covered the birds' legs. In 1845, Cochins were exhibited at London's first major poultry show, held in Regents Park Zoo. Five years later, at a poultry show in Birming-

According to the Zohar, an ancient Jewish mystical text, "When God visits Paradise each midnight to confer with the souls of the pious, all the trees break out in adoration and their song awakens the cock, which in turn begins to praise God, at the same time calling upon men to praise the Lord."

Luxury chicken coops
Queen Victoria's chickens lived in the lap of luxury. Her "poultry house" resembled a country manor more than a chicken coop.

Cochin crazy

The English Cochin obsession—which afflicted the entire country in the mid 1850s—was aptly named "The Poultry Mania" by the popular satirical magazine Punch. *Punch's chicken cartoons appeared often throughout this era, poking light-hearted fun at the sillier mores of the chicken world.*

In 1569, Prudent Choyselat wrote *Le Discourse Economique*, a French book devoted entirely to the subject of chickens. In it he urges a friend to consider raising chickens and describes the fortune to be made with a small investment of poultry and two acres of land. The book was translated into English in 1580 and is considered the first English book devoted to poultry husbandry.

ham, tens of thousands of gawkers became instant poultry fanciers. Poultry shows became the rage and attracted crowds so large they blocked the surrounding streets.

England became "Cochin Crazy," and fowl fancier Queen Victoria increased the excitement with her new flock of Cochins. Her poultry holdings consisted of half a dozen very extensive yards, several small fields, and numerous feeding and laying houses for winter use—an indication that her chickens lived in the lap of luxury. The Cochins sparked an avid interest in raising the birds among the landed gentry and middle-class farmers. Their popularity was enhanced not only because they were beautiful, but also because they were docile, easy to manage, indiscriminate eaters, and exceptional egg layers. The breed was also very maternal; Cochin hens often served as foster moms to motherless chicks.

The new obsession with raising comely clucks was accentuated when Queen Victoria banned cockfighting in 1849. The gentry diverted its attention from breeding battling birds to creating pure pampered poultry for exhibition purposes. Hundreds of pounds sterling were paid for a single Cochin. *Punch* tells of a Cochin costing more than £1,000, an outrageous sum even now.

The first English poultry club was formed in 1864, and the first "standards of perfection" were drafted the next year.

American Chickens

The American chicken industry has come a long way since the colonists arrived in Jamestown, Virginia, in 1607. Except for fighting cocks, the birds were considered inferior to other domestic animals, perhaps because they were often leftover provisions from the voyage. In Jamestown in 1609, there were a reported 500 chickens, most of which were eaten during the colony's famine later that year. The flock was replenished the next year when ships arrived with new settlers and provisions.

For the next 250 years or so, raising chickens was a casual pastime, a job usually left to women and children. For the most part, the chickens were not housed or even fed. They coexisted with other animals, living on leftovers and what Mother Nature could provide for them. They slept in trees, and their eggs had to be hunted, often by children. On an average, hens laid only about thirty eggs a year, and farm wives often sold the eggs as a small source of income—hence the term "egg money."

In the 1800s, interest in breeding expanded and new American breeds were developed. Some of the first were Dominiques, Plymouth Rocks, Rhode Island Reds, and Wyandottes. Then, as in England when the Cochins arrived in 1843, an interest became an obsession, and raising fancy fowl became a popular pastime.

One of the first poultry books in the United States, entitled the *American Poulterer's Companion*, was written in 1843 by C. N. Bement under the pen name of M. R. Cock. (I am the proud owner of a beautiful 1867 edition that I bought in New York City. When I purchased it, the shop owner said with amazement, "I never thought I would sell this book!")

The first "Exhibition of Fancy Poultry in the United States of America" was held in 1849 and truly launched the American poultry industry. Organized by a Boston doctor, John C. Bennett, this prestigious gathering at Boston's Quincy Market attracted more than ten thousand people from every walk of life, including such dignitaries as noted orator and politician Daniel Webster, a breeder of Java fowls. Showing their beauties were 219 exhibitors, who displayed 1,023 chickens of many breeds.

George P. Burnham, a poultry breeder in the United States, and Queen Victoria exchanged gifts of Cochins. In his humorous 1855 book, *The History of the Hen Fever*, Burnham described Americans as being afflicted with a made-up disease. This perceived illness was marked by an obsession with fancy fowl, the creation of numerous poultry societies (including one Burnham called "The Mutual Admiration Society of Hen Men"), and outlandish

Formed in 1918, the New York State Co-operative Official Poultry Breeders is one of the oldest poultry improvement associations in the United States. The organization's 1933 yearbook is an interesting testimonial to the popularity of the White Leghorn. There is barely a mention of any other breed. More than 100 certified Leghorn breeders are listed in the co-op, compared with only a handful raising Rhode Island Reds, Plymouth Rocks, and Wyandottes. Many of the breeders boasted that their stock laid more than 300 eggs per year. The champion recorded 355.

THE HISTORY
OF
THE HEN FEVER.
A Humorous Record.
BY
GEO. P. BURNHAM.

In one Volume.==Illustrated

BOSTON:
JAMES FRENCH AND COMPANY.
NEW YORK: J. C. DERBY.
PHILADELPHIA: T. B. PETERSON.

Hen Fever
In 1855, George P. Burnham wrote The History of the Hen Fever, *a humorous satire complete with cartoons, on the obsessiveness of chicken fanciers in the United States at that time.*

The first commercial shipment of baby chickens was sent from Stockton, New York, to Chicago in 1892.

Lunch counter

A farm wife feeds a flock of handsome Barred Plymouth Rocks in 1937. Feeding chickens and gathering eggs were chores that often fell to women and children on American farms. (Photograph © J. C. Allen & Son, Inc.)

prices for prized chickens—up to $150 for a pair of Cochins. Even P.T. Barnum of circus fame got into the act and organized the first national poultry show in New York in 1854.

One of the first poultry censuses, taken in 1880, determined that there were 102 million chickens in the United States. A decade later there were 258 million.

Cornell University offered the first course in poultry husbandry in 1891. By 1920, there were sixty-five colleges and experimental stations involved in poultry research. In 1916, sixty-one poultry magazines existed. A flood of pamphlets extolled all manner of breeding and raising techniques, feed, and supplies.

Toward the end of the nineteenth century, nearly all respectable farmers owned fancy fowl, but many farm communities developed their own strains of Rocks or Leghorns. During this period, selective breeding and specialization in both egg production or meat production also drew attention. Good layers were now in great demand, with competitions popping up around the country to determine the most prolific breeds. Some of the first contests were held at Kansas State College in 1904 and in Storrs, Connecticut, in 1911.

The winner of these contests was the Leghorn strains, and America's love affair with the breed, often referred to as "The Egg Machine," began. The birds originated in Leghorn, Italy, but were perfected in the United States, England, and Denmark. They were everything the breeders needed. Hens laid abundant eggs, were hearty, and weren't "broody" (meaning they didn't have a strong desire to nest and thus temporarily stop laying eggs).

In the early twentieth century, raising chickens was still primarily a side business run by wives, with the help of children. Land, feed, and labor were affordable, and little capital was needed. Compared with crop farming, chicken raising was much less labor intensive. In 1910, there were 5 million farmers, who averaged 80.4 chickens per farm. Even in urban areas, there was one chicken for every two persons. The average egg consumption exceeded 300 eggs a year.

The U.S. egg industry received a tremendous boost during World War I as the demand for eggs increased. More and more people got into the business, and chicken farms increased their productivity. But there was a downside to all this growth. Labor prices increased, land values rose, and the delicate balance between expenses and profit was at the mercy of fluctuating market forces. When the war ended, there were too many egg farmers, with overproduction decreasing egg prices. The importing of eggs from China had become a serious problem to American farmers, who lobbied for tariffs on the imported eggs. Throughout the country, poultry cooperatives were established to protect the farmers from the manipulation of egg prices by wholesalers. Among the cooperatives was the 5,500-member Poultry Producers of Central California, organized in 1916. The cooperative helped stabilize the price of eggs nationwide and safeguarded farmers from exploitation. By 1920, the chicken business was again looking hopeful.

At this time, raising chickens for meat gained popularity. Success stories, such as that of Mrs. Wilmer Steele, inspired a new wave of chicken farmers. Mrs. Steele was from Delmarva Peninsula near Chesapeake Bay. She purchased 500 chickens in 1923 and sold them for sixty-two cents per pound live weight (the equivalent of five dollars

The Democratic Rooster

The rooster has often served as the symbol of the Democratic Party. The association began in 1840 in Greenfield, Indiana, with a technique for delivering political rhetoric called "crowing." This act was made popular by a representative in the Indiana General Assembly, Joseph Chapman, an effective public speaker known for his "crowing" ability to stir up Democratic support against the rival Whigs. The slogan "Crow Chapman Crow" became a popular, powerful slogan for the Democrats in 1840 during Martin Van Buren's second presidential campaign. Although Van Buren lost to William Harrison, the Indiana Democrats adopted the rooster as their emblem, and before long, the rooster was accepted and recognized as the emblem of the national Democratic Party.

During the 1844 presidential election, the rooster symbol contributed to candidate James K. Polk's name recognition and ultimate victory. In 1884, the rooster helped Grover Cleveland score a victory. In 1968, when George C. Wallace ran for president as an independent, he co-opted the Democratic rooster, saying, "In Alabama, the state Democratic Party makes the rules, not the national party." Although the rooster was later ousted by the donkey as the national party's mascot, the rooster is still a powerful symbol and is reported to remain the official party emblem on several state ballots.

"And the winner is . . ."

Egg-laying contests were extremely popular in the United States beginning in the early 1900s, and the winners fetched handsome prizes. (Publisher: International Stock Food Co., Minnesota Historical Society)

per pound in today's market). With prices like this to attract breeders, it wasn't long before chicken was second only to corn as a revenue-producer for rural homes.

In 1928, just before the Great Depression, the Republicans—particularly presidential candidate Herbert C. Hoover—promised to put "a chicken in every pot" as the United States economy began to sour. This promise won Hoover the election.

As with its terrible predecessor, World War II was also good for the chicken industry. The troops needed to be fed, and military demand for dried and powdered eggs was high. After the war, raising poultry became an American dream. Following the Depression's hard times and the war's horror, people yearned for a simpler life. In 1943, there were 12,000 hatcheries in the United States (up from fifty in 1909). But getting into the chicken business was not for the faint hearted. Cutthroat competition and increased cost for new technology, including air conditioning units, conveyor belts for feed and collecting eggs, and watering and waste disposal systems, made it nearly impossible for the small farmer to survive. Lack of space became another problem after the war, as farm land was gobbled up by developers. Neighbors resented chickens and their malodor. The birds were voted out of urban areas, land prices increased, and farmers were forced to move farther away from the city.

By the 1940s, there were large breeding and egg-laying operations that each had as many as 100,000 hens hard at work. By the end of the 1950s, the smaller poultry keepers were faced with rising land prices, higher taxes, higher labor cost, disease, and increased cost of equipment. By 1960, the small-time poultry farm was all but extinct.

Yet a handful of astute chicken farmers survived the demands of scale. Perdue Farms was started by Arthur Perdue in 1920 with a mere twenty-three pullets and a chicken coop. His son, Frank, made the company into a household name in the early 1970s by using a television media blitz to sell his birds and eggs. Jim Perdue, Frank's son and Arthur's grandson, now runs the family's Maryland poultry company and continues the tradition of savvy advertising (see chapter 5).

Today, the chicken industry is very competitive, with a small fluctuation in the price of eggs or meat translating into millions of dollars of gain or loss per year. According to the National Chicken Council, the poultry-procession portion of the industry, including retail, restaurants, and exports, generates $40 billion in sales a year.

The Petaluma Story

From the early 1900s until the 1940s, Petaluma, California, was one of the nation's leading chicken centers. Its location near a busy seaport about forty miles north of San Francisco, its climate, and its soil helped to enhance its allure. Immigrants from Russia, Germany, Sweden, Denmark, Ireland, Italy, and Japan came in droves to make their chicken fortunes. In 1910, Petaluma claimed to be "the largest poultry center in the world." It later claimed the title of "the egg basket of the world." By 1917, Petaluma was the international leader of the chicken and egg industry, and the city began celebrating its success with a National Egg Day and parade in 1918.

Chicken-related enterprises flourished in Petaluma, including feed mills, packing plants, lumberyards, incubator and brooder manufacturers, publishers of poultry material, hardware stores, cage makers, and companies to transport the chickens. Dr. James E. Keyes moved to Petaluma from Pennsylvania and established the world's only chicken pharmacy, catering to and alleviating fowl diseases.

Two visionaries, Isaac Dias and Lyman Byce, joined forces to create a viable incubator, one capable of hatching up to 650 eggs. They formed the Petaluma Incubator Company in the late 1800s. Christopher Nisson, who moved to Petaluma from Denmark, was among the first to realize the incubator's potential and created Nisson's Pioneer Hatchery, the first commercial hatchery on the West Coast. Others followed. During the 1920s, California had 262 commercial hatcheries, 17 of which were in Petaluma.

The establishment of the Petaluma and Santa Rosa Electric Railway in 1903 helped to centralize Petaluma's chicken community. Called the Chicken and Cow Line, the railway ran for thirty-seven miles, bringing supplies to farmers and carrying their produce to the depot.

Many factors led to the demise of the Petaluma poultry craze. By the end of the 1940s, chicken farmers in Petaluma were facing the same dismal situation as those in the rest of the country. As the twentieth century progressed, technology and expensive equipment made it more difficult for the small farmer to exist. The third generation chicken farmers wanted nothing to do with the hard labor and small profits. Land values rose in the Petaluma area, tempting farmers to sell their property to developers, and as the suburbs encroached, stinky chickens were no longer welcome. The development of tasty new and well-publicized cereals and the promotion of healthy nutrition habits made the old-fashioned bacon-and-egg breakfast less appealing. Even the invention of the pneumatic tire took its toll on the situation, as the Petaluma riverboat delivery system was challenged by more efficient truck transportation.

Today, Petaluma is a charming town but sadly lacking in chickens.

Egg protest

This early-1900s postcard reflects the growing dissatisfaction of egg-producing farmers on egg importation, primarily from China, which drove down the price of eggs.

More than 9 million chickens were destroyed in California alone when a Newcastle disease epidemic broke out in 1972.

It is reported that Tyson Foods, the company of Arkansas chicken mega-mogul Don Tyson, butchers 150 million chickens a week, making the company the largest poultry-processing plant in the United States.

In the 1920s, an American family could live comfortably on a two-acre farm with a few hundred chickens. That same standard of living today takes hundreds of thousands of chickens

The Chicken as Industry

> Of all feathered animals, there is none more useful than the common hen. Her eggs supply us with food during her life, and her flesh affords us delicate meat after her death. What a motherly care does she take of her young. How closely and tenderly does she watch over them, and cover them with her wings: and how bravely does she defend them from every enemy, from which she herself would fly away in terror, if she had not them to protect!

Who would have guessed that the simple hen, so aptly described in 1836 by the Reverend C. S. Lovell's *Young Pupils' Second Book*, would become the object of a multi-billion dollar industry?

The development of the U.S. poultry industry paralleled the development of heavy manufacturing in urban centers. Beginning in the mid 1800s, industry evolved from traditional cottage-style businesses or small factories into large-scale productions. Much of the population was forced to move into cities for better paying jobs, and the new city dwellers had to purchase eggs and meat, rather than relying on their own supply. The remaining farmers were poorly equipped to handle the situation, because they lacked the knowledge to produce and handle large numbers of poultry products. The challenge was augmented by poor roads and inadequate transportation facilities, both of which delayed massive shipments of farm goods to city markets.

To capitalize on this opportunity to attract new—and hungry—consumers, farmers turned to science and technology to increase their profits. The goal was simply to produce bigger chickens faster and to increase egg supply. The hen was moved inside, because uniformity in growth, laying, and egg quality could be better achieved in a controlled environment. The move eliminated the need to hunt for eggs and the risk of losing them (or the chickens) to predators. The hen was no longer able to relax under a shady bush, take dust baths, wander around searching for insects and worms, engage in chicken sex, or take care of her young. She was housed together with other hens in coops or on her own in a small cage, where she was given carefully controlled food, water, and light. Conveyor belts took away her eggs. "Lay or Bust" was her raison d'etre. No sir, it was not fun being a chicken anymore, except for the fact that she was afforded protection, her needs were met, and she no longer had to worry about Rocky Raccoon.

In 1934, John Kimber started a hatchery in Fremont, California, which he called Kimber Farms. Actually, it wasn't a farm at all. Instead, it was a vast, sterile laboratory run by a new type of farmer: the white-coated specialist. The chickens received numbers, such as K-22 and K-43, instead of names. The goal was to improve and control the quality of eggs by increasing the thickness of their shells and creating eggs of uniform size, shape, and color. This goal led to the hybridization of the White Leghorn breed. Although hybridizing chickens caused even more disease on occasion, the sterile environment managed to create a truly efficient and affordable chicken.

Incubators and Hatcheries

Spring shipment
A 1920s farmer and his wife prepare to send dozens of flats of chicks to farms across the country, in this photo from the U.S. Department of Agriculture.

Any farmer who wants lots of eggs does not like broody hens. A broody chicken is one who is stubbornly maternal, wanting to sit on and hatch her eggs. Since eggs take twenty-one days to hatch, the hen would be out of commission for two to four months before she was ready to lay again. Hence, the incubator.

Incubators were used in China and Egypt before the time of Christ, but it was not until the nineteenth century that the devices were used commercially. Although many individuals later patented various types of incubators, the first marketable incubator was displayed in London in 1839 by William Bucknell. A few years later, in 1843, a patent was granted to Napoleon Guerin for an American-made incubator, and another one to Jacob Graves in 1873.

Thomas D. Wilson of New Jersey was one of the first breeders to incubate, market, and sell baby chickens in the United States, beginning in 1892. He built his own incubator, which could handle up to 400 eggs for local sales. When he realized that baby chickens could live without food or water for thirty-six hours after hatching, he started shipping them by rail as far as Chicago. Thus the U.S. hatchery business began. In 1918, there were 250 hatcheries in the United States and more than 10,000 by 1927, artificially incubating more than one half of the baby chickens raised in the country.

Chapter 2

Real Chickens

To all but the experts, identifying chickens is daunting—especially when you consider that there are hundreds of breeds, each with numerous varieties. Some breeds are easy to pick out. The Polish, one of my favorites, has a puffy feather-do. The Spanish has a striking white mask. Japanese long-tails, with their twenty-foot dorsal feathers, and Cochins, with their big "hairy" legs, are both easy to spot. All chickens have a basic structure of head, comb, wattles, beak, hackles, and feathering. It is the subtle variations—such as the size, shape, and angle of the tail; the conformation of the comb and the number of points on it; or the different feather types and colors that make knowing and identifying all breeds a task best left to the pros.

Different breeds of chickens exist for many reasons. Some breeds are fast growers and excellent meat birds. Others are prolific and precocious egg layers. There are also "fancy fowl" and fighting cocks.

On one end of the chicken-breeding spectrum is the multi-billion-dollar chicken industry, a high-tech, fiercely competitive business where breeding is done with scientific precision and an eye toward marketing. On the other extreme, there are people like me, who raise chickens for the sheer pleasure of their company, plus the bonus of a steady supply of fresh eggs and an occasional fresh chicken for the pot. In between are varying degrees of enthusiasts, including poultry fanciers who raise chickens for competition. Valuable show birds are preened for the dazzling good looks that could garner a blue ribbon. Their color, size, feathers, combs, tails, and legs must conform to strict standards of perfection for the all-knowing poultry judges.

In addition to the above, farmers still keep chickens as a side business or a source for personal consumption, and youngsters also raise chickens for school or 4-H projects. And, despite the animal rights lobby, cockfighting is still prevalent throughout the world, and roosters are raised for endurance, stamina, and a garrulous nature.

Facing page:
Gold on gold
A handsome "buff" rooster wallows amidst the golden sunflowers. (Photograph © Lynn M. Stone)

Inset:
Circus chickens
Silkies were exploited as "freak" chickens, as evidenced by this early-twentieth-century sideshow banner by Fred Johnson.

The American chicken industry is valued at $40 billion, including retail, restaurant, and export businesses, according to the National Chicken Council.

In 1873, the American Poultry Association was organized in Buffalo, New York. The purpose of the organization was "to standardize the varieties of domestic fowl so that a fair decision could be made as to which qualities marked prize winners." Prizewinners, quite naturally, fetched a pretty penny. A year later, the first *American Standard of Excellence,* now known as the *American Standard of Perfection,* was adopted.

According to the *American Standard,* we can divide the chicken world into two principal sections: Large Fowl and Bantams. In general, the categories are the same. It is only the size that differs, the bantams being a diminutive version of the large fowl, about one-fourth to one-fifth the size of their large counterparts. In the 1874 *Standard,* there were forty-one breeds or varieties of chickens. In the 1998 edition of the *American Standard of Perfection,* there were fifty-three breeds of large fowl and sixty-one breeds of bantams as well as their many varieties. The popularity of bantams has greatly increased for many reasons; because they are smaller than the large fowl, bantams are cheaper to feed and more easily transported to shows, but their egg supply is just as prolific.

There are six categories of large fowl, based on the region of origin: American, Asiatic, English, Mediterranean, Continental, and a miscellaneous category called All Others. The bantam classes are a little more complicated. They are divided into five classes: Game Bantams, Single Comb Clean Legged Other Than Game Bantams, Rose Comb Clean Legged Bantams, All Other Combs Clean Legged, and Feather Legged. Then, in many cases, there are varying colors and different standard feather patterns within a breed. For example, there are seven different classes of the Plymouth Rock due to varying colors. Furthermore, some of the breeds have different comb styles. The subtleties differentiating the chicken breeds are often slight. A new breed cannot exist until strict rules are observed over many years.

Given how many chicken breeds and variations there are just in the United States, not to mention around the world, it would be impossible to describe them all here. The following are some that have a special place in my heart, while others are of historical importance.

Know your combs

The comb's conformation and number of points differs greatly from breed to breed. Pictured: 1. Single, 2. Pea, 3. Walnut, 4. Rose, 5. Rose, 6. V-shaped, 7. Buttercup, 8. Strawberry.

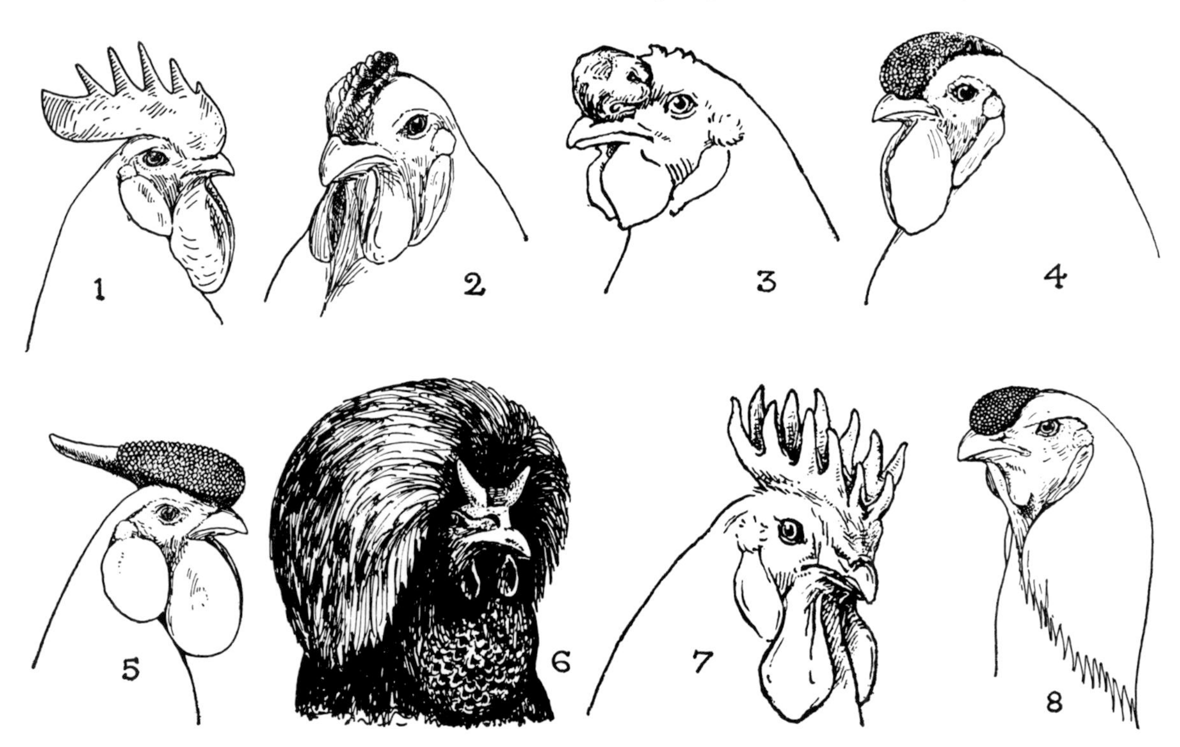

Japanese Bantam

This Black Tailed White Japanese Bantam appears at peace with the world. The Japanese chickens exist only in the Bantam category. Other varieties include Black, Black Tailed Buff, Gray, Mottled, and White. The rooster sports a flamboyant tail, while the hen's plumage is less showy. (Photograph © Lynn M. Stone)

Spanish chickens
Both the White-faced Black Spanish and the Blue Andalusian hail from Spain. According to the American Standard, *the White-faced Black Spanish is probably the oldest breed in the Mediterranean class. Both breeds have white faces although the Andalusian's is much less pronounced. Each breed comes in only one variety, and both were admitted to the first* Standard *in 1874. (Color photograph © Lynn M. Stone)*

Araucana

Araucanas hail from South America and, as noted in chapter 1, are perhaps an old breed of chicken. They were discovered by missionaries in Chile in 1560 and by the Spaniards in Mexico in the 1500s. According to the British Araucana Society, they were brought to England in the early 1920s, and soon afterwards, they made their way to the United States. Araucanas are known for their beautiful eggs of varying colors, from blue, turquoise, and deep olive to different shades of tan. Araucanas have ear tufts protruding from the sides of their necks. They are also described as "rumpless"—they were bred to be tail-less to make it more difficult for foxes to catch them. In the 1970s, a variation of the Araucana, called the Ameraucana, was developed in the United Sates for its blue eggs and to be a better meat bird. Unlike their ancestors, Ameraucanas sport tail feathers. The Araucana was admitted to the *Standard* in 1976, and the Ameraucana in 1984.

Poised and ready for action

The Ameraucana is a breed linked to the Aruacana from South America and known for its beautiful bluish-green eggs. The birds were bred to retain the beautiful egg color with an improved meat quality. (Photograph © Lynn M. Stone)

Spanish conquistador Hernando Cortes found chickens in Mexico when he invaded the country in 1520. When the conquistadors invaded what is now New Mexico in the mid 1500s, they brought chickens with them.

Australorp

The Australorp, a descendant of the English Black Orpington, was developed in Australia. The goal was to develop a new breed of chicken that was a prolific egg layer, yet retained the meat quality of the Orpington. Australorp roosters are quite hefty, weighing up to eight pounds. The breed was introduced to the United States in the 1920s and admitted to the *Standard* in 1929. Australorps are black with a brilliant green sheen.

Barnvelder

Barnvelders are originally from the district of Barneveld in Holland, home of the Dutch Poultry Museum and one of the major chicken centers of the world. Developed as a breed in the mid 1800s and known for their prolific production of rather large brown eggs, they are the most famous breed of the Netherlands. They were admitted to the *Standard* in 1991.

Brahma

Both the Light and Dark Brahmas were admitted to the *Standard* in 1874. They were originally called Chittagongs, Gray Shanghais, and Brahma Pootras, later shortened to Brahmas. They hail from the banks of the Brahmaputra, a river in Assam, India. The bird was first brought to New York by a sailor in 1850 and created quite a stir because of its interesting appearance. Brahmas can grow as tall as thirty inches, and they sport a pea-shaped comb. Like the Cochins, they have feathered legs that have the appearance of being hairy. There was much debate about whether Cochins and Brahmas were the same variety, but it was widely held that the birds were a cross of Malays and Cochins.

Buckeye

There are diverse opinions on where this breed originated. The popular belief is that it came from Bucks County, Pennsylvania, even though the 1998 *Standard* stated it originated in Ohio, the Buckeye State. Other experts say the bird got its name from its coloring, which is similar to that of the buckeye nut. The Buckeye was admitted to the *Standard* in 1904. According to the *American Poulterer's Companion* (1867), the breed didn't have too much going for it. The hens laid a few large and well-flavored eggs of dark cinnamon color but were great eaters, poor layers, and miserable sitters, seldom producing more than twelve or fifteen eggs before they became broody. Currently, they are often profitable for making capons.

Chantecler

The Chantecler is a true Canadian breed. Admitted to the *Standard* in 1921, it was developed between 1908 and 1918 by a Trappist monk at the Oka Agricultural Institute in Quebec by crossing various breeds. The goal was to create a vigorous chicken, one able to survive in the harsh Canadian climate. The result was a good winter layer that has a reduced comb and wattles, which offer less surface for potential frostbite.

Facing page:
Catching the breeze
This beautiful Brahma appears to be in a state of reflection—perhaps thinking back to his Asian roots. Formerly known as the Chittagong, Gray Shanghai, and Brahma Pootra, its name was shortened to Brahma. The breed arrived in England with the Cochins in the 1840s. There are three varieties: the Light and Dark were admitted to the Standard *in 1874; the Buff was accepted in 1924. (Photograph © Lynn M. Stone)*

Crevecoeur

The Crevecoeur is one of the oldest of French breeds, a rare breed that originated in Normandy. There is not much information regarding their origin; however, Darwin classified them as subvarieties of the Polish, along with the Houdan. The Crevecoeur made the American Standard *in 1874. (Photograph © Lynn M. Stone)*

Cochin

In the 1600s, missionaries who traveled throughout China found extremely large chickens, presumably Cochins, raised by a religious sect called the Brahmo-Buddhists. The eggs were sold to help support the monastery, and the meat was shared with visitors. As noted in chapter 1, the Cochins' arrival in England in 1843 caused quite a stir. Cochin varieties include Partridge, Buff, White, and Black.

Cochins are sweet and maternal. The one I owned, named Thunder Thighs, disappeared one day, and I sadly surmised that she had been a feast for the raccoons. Happily, she had instead sneaked off and proudly reappeared one day with a brood of eight little Cochins.

Cornish

Originally known as Indian Game, the Cornish originated in Cornwall, England, in the early 1820s. It is a composite of many different bloodlines, including the Aseel, the Black Red Old English, and the Malay. Cornishes come in four varieties: Dark, White, White Laced Red, and Buff. Unlike most breeds, male and female Cornishes have the same body type. Typically, the rooster is larger, with a more spectacular tail and larger comb and wattles. Despite the Cornishes' pugnacious appearance, they were never fighting cocks. They are, however, one of the most popular commercial hybrids, and due to their rapid growth and large breasts, many of them are found on dining room tables.

I raised a batch of twenty-five Cornishes only once. They are big, fat, lazy birds that have only one thing on their mind—eating. Many chose not to even go outside to free range, preferring to sit around and be fed. Though they did grow at a rapid rate, their legs could hardly support their bulbous weight, and many died mysteriously.

Cubalaya

Yes, the Cubalaya was developed in Cuba, although its ancestors came from the Philippine Islands. The Cubalaya was first exhibited in the United States in 1939 and accepted into the *American Standard* that same year. The birds are quite rare now and seldom exhibited in the United States.

Something to crow about

Cubalayas were bred in Cuba from a variety of breeds and are still plentiful there. The Black Breasted Red variety, shown here, was admitted to the Standard *in 1939 along with the White and Black Cubalayas. They are not plentiful in the United States today. (Photograph © Lynn M. Stone)*

Delaware

Delawares were developed in Delaware in 1940, the product of Barred Plymouth Rock males and New Hampshire females. For some genetic reason, they are almost all white, with a bit of black barred feathers on their hackles and tail. Another interesting genetic trait is that when a Delaware hen is crossed with a New Hampshire or Rhode Island Red rooster, the sex of their offspring may be determined by color: The males have the hen's Delaware pattern, and the females have the solid red feather pattern of the rooster. This certainly makes sexing the chicks easy!

Delaware
Delawares were developed in the 1940s in the First State. They have only black and white feathers. There is only one variety of Delaware, and the breed was admitted to the Standard *in 1952. (Photograph © Lynn M. Stone)*

Training Chickens

"Smile for the judges"
A young woman teaches her White Wyandotte how to pose properly in preparation for a 1920s poultry show. Chickens are judged not only for their pulchritude, but also their behavior. Each chicken is handled by the judges and must behave.

Contrary to popular belief, chickens are not only reasonably smart but also extremely trainable.

In the 1940s, psychologists Marian and Keller Breland studied under B. F. Skinner, a noted psychologist of human behavior who purported that positive feedback at each stage of development created a desired behavior. The Brelands applied the repetition-and-reward method of training to animals, a technique called "operant conditioning." They used this technique in a company they formed in 1943 called Animal Behavior Enterprises (ABE). In 1950, they moved the operation to Hot Springs, Arkansas, where they opened the I.Q. Zoo, a tourist attraction and learning center. Their work attracted such notables as Walt Disney and Marlin Perkins, host of the television program *Mutual of Omaha's Wild Kingdom*. The couple often used chickens to demonstrate their methods.

After Keller died in 1965, Marian later married Bob Bailey, who had been in charge of the U.S. Navy's Dolphin Training Program and also worked at ABE. They continued to expand the operation and in 1996 began offering classes in animal training, again using the chicken as the star model. They trained chickens for commercials, animal shows, and behavioral research. They also took their school on the road, traveling coast to coast with a trailer full of trained chickens.

Terry Ryan, owner of Legacy, Inc. in Washington State, offers "Chicken Camp" as part of her dog training school. She claims that chickens are smart and respond well to handling and food. Her favorite breeds to train are Cochins, Silkies, and Sebrights, although other trainers swear by White Leghorns. Chickens have been taught to pull a little wagon, discriminate between colors and shapes, pull a string to trigger a gun, and dance.

Delaware is often referred to as the little "Blue Hen" state, and the athletic teams for the University of Delaware are known as the Fightin' Blue Hens.

Delaware Blue Hens are not an official breed but a variety of fighting game cocks. The nickname refers to fighting regiment that was famous during the Revolutionary War. In 1775, under the command of Captain John Caldwell, the company of Kent County soldiers became known as the Sons of the Blue Hen. The reason, some say, is that Captain Caldwell was a fan of cockfighting and carried two cocks onto the battlefield. Another theory says the soldiers themselves were known for conducting cockfights between battles. A third theory argues that the men looked like chickens in their blue coats, leather hats with high peaks, and red feather plumes.

Whatever the truth, on April 14, 1939, the "Blue Hen Chicken" was voted the official Delaware state bird.

In the mood

This Dominique rooster is in the mood to mate. He is doing his little dance to attract a hen. However, the ladies in the background look a bit blasé. Only time will tell if they succumb to his desires. (Photograph © Lynn M. Stone)

Dominique

Dominiques are considered among the oldest of the distinctive American breeds and were in the first *Standard* in 1874. According to the *American Poulterer's Companion* (1867), although the Dominique is old and distinct, "it is generally looked upon as mere 'farmyard fowl,' that is the accidental result of promiscuous crossing." Called great "all-round fowl," they are reputed to be excellent layers, very hardy, and tasty. Their plumage is a beautiful slate color, and their feathers are barred with black and white.

Dorking

In A.D. 30, the Roman writer Columella described Dorkings as square in shape with short sturdy legs and five toes. Pliny the Elder and Aristotle also mention Dorkings in their writings. The birds were brought to South Britain in 55 B.C. and developed there. At that time, the ancient Britons did not eat fowl, but the Romans introduced them to dining on Dorking. The breed became the first table bird in merrie olde Britain.

In Search of the Perfect Poulet

My husband and I went to France in 2000 in search of the perfect *poulet*. We found it—a breed called Poulet de Bresse, raised in a region between Paris and Lyon called Bourg-en-Bresse. Touted by gourmands to be the Rolls Royce of poulet, Poulet de Bresse have been around since the sixteenth century, as shown by a reference in the municipal records of the village of Bourg-en-Bresse in 1591. These beautiful and tasty fowl are as French as can be and sport the French national colors: red (comb), white (body), and blue (legs). Jean Anthelme Brillat-Savarin, well-known gourmet and author of *The Physiology of Taste*, referred to their succulent flesh in 1825. Ernest Hemingway spoke of Poulet de Bresse with reverence and suggested serving them with truffles. Today, they are served in the finest French restaurants and sold for pricey figures in the boisterous markets. Like fine French wine, Poulet de Bresse is strictly controlled by government standards, and each chicken is sold with a seal of authenticity called an *appelation contrôlée*, which guarantees that it was fed a certain diet and raised in a particular manner. All I can say is that Poulet de Bresse, however cooked, are *magnifique*!

Poulet de Bresse
This photo was taken on a farm in Bourg-en-Bresse, France, where my husband and I stayed. We were in search of the "perfect poulet" and found it in this breed. These birds are not only blessed with good genes, but they are also raised in a very specific manner with a strict diet and other regulations. They are guaranteed with an appellation contrôlée, *which assures their authenticity and justifies their steep price. (Photograph by Martin Hintz)*

The frizzy Frizzle

Frizzles appear to be in a constant need of a beautician. Their feathers are twisted, like cowlicks. The Frizzle was admitted to the Standard *in 1874. Today, in both the Large Fowl category and the Bantam, Frizzles may compete in any of the classes or breeds. (Photograph © Lynn M. Stone)*

Frizzle

Frizzles seem to be continually having a bad hair day, with cowlicks, twisted hackles, and feathers curling backwards. Little is known about their origin, although Charles Darwin identified them as "Frizzled or Caffie Fowls." They are mostly bred for exhibition, although they can be good egg producers.

Hamburg

Though the name of the breed is German, Hamburgs are originally Dutch. There are six varieties, all admitted to the *Standard* in 1874: Silver Spangled, Golden Spangled, Golden Penciled, Silver Penciled, White, and Black. They are beautiful exhibition birds and prolific egg layers—in fact, they were called the "Dutch Everyday Layer."

Faverolle

Faverolles were developed by crossing Houdans, Dorkings, and Asiatics. Admitted to the American Standard *in 1914, they were bred for winter egg laying and as a large table fowl. The varieties are Salmon and White. (Artwork © Diane Jacky)*

Chickens can live more than ten years, although it is rare to find a teenage chicken.

Larger than life

This Jersey Giant surveys the horizon, knowing he is a gargantuan in the chicken world. The cock weighs up to thirteen pounds and the hen up to ten. The two varieties—Black and White—were developed in New Jersey in the 1880s. (Photograph © Lynn M. Stone)

Ready for the harvest

This Lakenvelder rooster hails from Germany and Holland, established there by the 1830s. They have only black and white feathers in both the Large Fowl and Bantam category. (Photograph © Lynn M. Stone)

Lakenvelder

Lakenvelder fowl made their first appearance in England in 1901. Traced back to the early 1800s in Germany and Holland, they were recognized in the United States in the 1930s. They are beautiful, with black and white feathers and slate legs. They were admitted to the *Standard* in 1939.

I had a bad experience with Lakenvelders. A hatch produced too many roosters, which then formed a "gang" and started to bully the other chickens. They reminded me of the classic image of '60s "hoods." I pictured them hunkered behind the barn in black leather jackets, smoking and drinking. One day they murdered my favorite rooster, a beautifully colored ten-year-old Leghorn. The Lakenvelders immediately went to the stew pot. They were delicious.

Long-tailed Chickens of Japan

The Phoenix and the Yokohama are breeds of long-tailed chickens from Japan. They are similar in appearance. In both breeds, the male's tail grows to three to four feet long, but the breeds' combs differ. The Phoenix sports a single comb as opposed to the walnut comb of the Yokohama. Both were admitted to the *American Standard* in the early 1980s.

The Tosa Onagadori is the true treasure of Japan. Breeder Reiman Takechi, who lived in Japan in the 1600s, developed this bird to please the shogun, who wanted long feathers to adorn his spears. The birds' incredible tails grew as long as fifteen feet, with the *Guinness Book of World Records* reporting one at thirty-four feet, nine and a half inches. Breeders keep the birds in special hutches, with perches high above the ground so the tails can be kept clean. When the bird is removed from its confines and permitted to walk around, its tail is coiled, suspended with a string, or carried by a handler. In 1923, the Tosa Onagadori were honored as a national treasure by the Japanese Ministry of Education.

The egg machine

In the early 1900s, White Leghorns, pronounced "legerns," became famous for their prolific egg-laying ability. In addition, they are not broody, a trait that appeals to farmers. Though there are sixteen different varieties, with not only different colors but also different combs, the White Leghorn is the most popular. (Photograph © J. C. Allen & Son, Inc.)

Leghorn

In the 1998 *American Standard,* there are sixteen varieties of Leghorns with varying colors and two different types of comb, the Single and the Rose. Though all Leghorns are good layers, the Single Comb White is the favored egg layer, able to lay more than 300 eggs a year. The White Leghorn arrived in the United States in 1828 and was shown at the 1849 Poultry Show. Charles H. Wycoff, a New York breeder, is given much credit for its popularity, by careful selection in the late 1800s. Many commercial hybrids evolved from this breed.

Modern Game

The Modern Game, also called Modern Exhibition Game, was created by breeders in Great Britain after cockfighting was banned there in 1849. It reached the height of its popularity in the late 1800s. Eight varieties of Games were admitted into the *American Standard* in 1874: Black Breasted Red, Brown Red, Golden and Silver Duckwings, Birchen, Red Pyle, White, and Black.

"Put all your eggs in the one basket
and watch that basket."
—Mark Twain (1835–1910),
The Tragedy of Pudd'nhead Wilson

Modern Game

This portrait by chicken artist Diane Jacky represents the ideal of the Modern Game. The breed was created as a result of the banning of cockfighting, after which the breeders concentrated on creating an exhibition bird. This curious-looking creature has extremely long legs, and its combs, wattles, and earlobes are "dubbed" or trimmed for show. (Artwork © Diane Jacky)

"I need a scarf"
Naked Necks are not blessed with neck plumage or typical chicken beauty. They are believed to have originated in either Hungary or Transylvania, a province of Romania, and perfected later in Germany. The breeding goal was a chicken with fewer feathers, making them easier to pluck. Beautiful or not, they were accepted into the Standard *in 1965. (Photograph © Lynn M. Stone)*

Naked Neck

Naked Necks, also known as Turkens or the Transylvanian Naked Necks, are not too popular, because—in all truth—they are quite ugly. They have a smooth neck that looks like a bad molt. Naked Necks are thought to have originated in eastern Hungary or Transylvania in Romania and became popular in Germany because—despite their unfortunate appearance—the areas of bare skin make them easy to dress. Although they have fewer than half the feathers of a normal chicken, they can withstand cold weather and are good egg layers. They are hardy and disease resistant.

Plymouth Rock

The Plymouth Rock was one of the first established breeds of poultry in the United States and was exhibited at the first poultry show in 1849. The Reverend D. A. Upham is credited with the creation of a new variety, the Barred Plymouth Rock by crossing a Black Cochin female or Black Java female and a Dominique male. The Barred Plymouth Rock made its debut at the Worcester, Massachusetts, poultry show in 1869 and was admitted to the 1874 *Standard of Excellence*. By 1882, according to *The Complete Poultry Book*, it was the most popular breed of fowl in the United States. The six other varieties of Plymouth Rocks—White, Buff, Silver Penciled, Partridge, Columbian, and Blue Plymouth—were established in various stages of the overall breed's development.

Polish

My favorite chickens are the Polish, not for their egg-laying ability or as a source of food but for their beautiful appearance and charming personalities. Despite its name, the breed is believed to have originated in Italy and were called Paduans by Aldrovandi. In England, the birds are called Polands. In Holland, they are referred to as Crested Dutch. The breed was developed in Holland in 1475, so the Dutch are given credit for its perfection. Also called "Top Knots," their beautiful head feathers grow from a knob on the top of their head.

I have owned several Polishes throughout the years, many of which hold a special place in my bank of fond chicken memories. Betty, a beautiful White Crested Black Polish, was the sole survivor of a weasel attack in which forty-nine of her siblings lost their lives. Forced to integrate into the social dynamic of the chicken coop as a youngster, Betty was the envy of mean-spirited hens that coveted her beautiful crown of head feathers. The birds proceeded to pluck Betty's head, leaving just a few feathery bangs drooping down her face. She then became Bald Betty. She and I were great friends. She loved to be held and petted, and she lived to a ripe old age of eight.

Where's the barber?
The Polish is characterized by a puffy hairdo, due to a protuberance or knot on the top of its head from which the feathers grow. This is a very sensitive area and caution must be taken not to touch the top of their heads. In the Large Fowl category, there are eight varieties—some with beards and others without. (Photograph © Thomas A. Schneider/Schneiderstock)

Rhode Island Red

The Rhode Island Red is truly an all-American breed of chicken. Developed in Little Compton, Rhode Island, in the 1800s, it is the official state bird. In Little Compton a stone wall with a bronze portrait of a

The Delicate Art of Chicken Sexing

Knowing a chicken's sex at birth is very important. Someone who wants an egg layer certainly doesn't want the hassle or expense of a randy rooster. At birth, to the untrained eye, hens and roosters have the same sexual apparatus, and their sex isn't apparent until they are five to six weeks old. But there exist highly skilled individuals called "chicken sexers," who glance at the underside of a chick to determine its sex.

This skill was developed in 1924 in Japan, where three scientists developed a technique for turning the chick's vent (rear end) inside out to expose the undeveloped sex organ. In 1933, the first Japanese chick sexers arrived in North America to train the locals in the new technique. A good chicken sexer, one who could sex 5,000 to 7,000 chicks a day, could fetch more than $4,000 a day plus expenses.

A steely-eyed Russian Orloff

Russian Orloffs are a very old Russian breed, descendants of Persian chickens. They have very small combs, perhaps developed to avoid frostbite in the harsh Russian winters. Now they are more popular in Germany, as well as Great Britain, France, and Denmark, than in Russia. (Photograph © Lynn M. Stone)

Rhode Island Red pays tribute to the breed. The birds are prolific egg layers of popular brown eggs. There are two varieties of Rhode Island Reds: the Single Comb, admitted to the *Standard* in 1904, and the Rose Comb, admitted in 1905. A new breed, the Rhode Island White, was admitted to the *Standard* in 1922.

Sebright

Sebrights are only a bantam breed. They were developed in England over a period of thirty years by Sir John Sebright. In 1815, he organized the Sebright Bantam Club. Golden and Silver Sebrights are very popular and were part of the first Standard in 1874.

Unfortunately, I had a bad Sebright experience. I owned a small but mighty Golden Sebright rooster who attacked me when I least expected. He leaped on my legs with claws extended—an indescribably frightening experience. I took to defending myself with a broom until my nerves could take no more and he was "sent away."

Shamo

Shamos (whose varieties are the Black, Black Breasted Red, and Wheaten) were originally brought to Japan in the seventeenth century for cockfighting, most likely because their fierce expressions were daunting to their opponents. Shamos are very tall and muscular, with slight plumage that barely covers their skin. Now they are known for their delicious meat quality and are protected birds in Japan.

Silkie

Silkies are unique in that their feathers feel like silk, hence the name. In his travel journals, Marco Polo (1254–1324?) described a black chicken that had fur like a cat, so it is often speculated that the Silkie originated in China. The Silkie is one of the breeds that only exist as bantams. There are twelve different varieties.

Sultan

Arriving in England from Istanbul in 1854, these glorious birds were called "Sultan's Fowl" in Turkey, where they were favorites of the royal court. The birds look like a combination of a Polish with a puffy hairdo and a Cochin with hairy legs. Sultans were admitted to the *Standard* in 1874.

He and she Sultans

Sultans are an old breed, arriving in England from Istanbul in the mid 1800s. They are striking, with a full head of upright feathers, a beard, whiskers, a muff, and feathered shanks. They also have five toes, rather than the usual four.

Wyandottes

Wyandottes were developed in New York in the late 1800s, the first being the Silver Laced. They were developed from a variety of breeds, and are noted for their full figure and a Rose Comb, which looks like a little flat hat. There are nine varieties, the Silver Laced referring to a particular type of feather.

Wyandotte

The original Wyandotte was the Silver Laced, developed by John P. Ray in New York in 1865. He combined the Sebright and the Cochin to produce this very hardy bird. It is tolerant of harsh weather and can lay eggs throughout the winter. It is believed that its name is derived from the Wyandotte Indians. Other varieties include the Golden Laced, White, Buff, Black, Partridge, Silver Pencilled, Columbian, and Blue.

Multicultural Clucks

From the object of superstition to a sacred image to a secular symbol, the chicken in social customs prevails around the world.

Throughout Africa, for example, customs and attitudes toward the chicken vary from tribe to tribe. The Azande tribe in the Sudan feeds a poison called benge to chickens. Benge, which is a substance related to strychnine, kills some chickens but does not affect others. At benge seances, a benge-fed chicken is asked questions, and the answer is determined by whether or not the bird lives.

Other African cultures regard the chicken as sacred and forbid the eating of eggs and birds. The Pondo raise chickens only for their feathers; the Nyoro use a cock as a morning wake-up call. Some cultures forbid women to eat chicken, fearing that it will cause promiscuity. In Algeria, an old custom said the sick could be cured by taking a cock to a spring, killing it, and wiping its blood on the face of the sick person.

In the royal court of Benin, a once-mighty military power in western Africa, roosters were held in high esteem. All levels of Benin society traditionally placed rooster figures on the graves of deceased mothers. Brass roosters were set on the ancestral altars of the Queen Mother and mothers of dignitaries, along with a dead fowl as a sacrificial offering. In other homes, altars to mothers of the living, as well as past household heads, were decorated with wooden roosters.

China has a long history of chicken rearing. Cockfighting was popular and chronicled well before the time of Christ. Chicken-shaped pottery, unearthed at an archeological dig in Jinshan province, dates back to 2700 B.C. In 2500 B.C., there was a government minister in charge of poultry raising. By the Shang Era (1520–1030 B.C.), the chicken was an important part of Chinese cuisine. Chinese writers refer to the operation of incubators as early as 1000 B.C.

The Chinese thought the rooster possessed the "Five Virtues" of literary accomplishment, martial spirit, courage, virtue, and loyalty. In art, the crown on its head portrays the literary spirit, and its spurs display a war-like character. In Chinese philosophy, the rooster was a symbol of one of the two life forces: yang, the masculine and positive principle in nature, which combines with yin, the female life force, to produce

Benin rooster

The Queen Mother plays an important role in the Benin kingdom. She is one of Benin's most powerful figures, and her authority equals that of the town chief. Upon her death, her grave is decorated with a rooster, a symbol of power and authority in the Benin culture. In this matriarchal society, women of more prominence had bronze, brass, or copper roosters adorning their graves, while women of lesser status had simple wooden roosters. This eighteen-inch-high bronze rooster from Benin is an example of a rooster made to honor a prominent Benin woman. (All rights reserved, The Metropolitan Museum of Art, Bequest of Mary Stillman Harkness, 1950. [50.145.47])

Postal chickens

The next Year of the Rooster in the Chinese zodiac 2005, which will hopefully yield a new crop of stamps with chicken images.

A hen never forgets him who stole her chickens. —African proverb

all that lives. The rooster represents the yang virtues of courage, benevolence, valor, and faithfulness.

The rooster is also the tenth symbolic animal in the twelve-year Chinese zodiac cycle. According to many myths and legends—Chinese, Indian, Korean, and Japanese—God (or Buddha) summoned all the animals on New Year's Day and promised each a reward. Only twelve showed up at the appointed time, and each was repaid by having a year named in its honor. In the twentieth century, those born in the years 1909, 1921, 1933, 1945, 1957, 1969, 1981, and 1993 are born in the Year of the Rooster. The first rooster year of the twenty-first century is 2005.

People born in rooster years are believed to possess certain characteristics relating to the animal. The cock is described as a pioneer in spirit, courageous, devoted to work and questing after knowledge, highly successful, direct and outspoken. On the downside, cocks are selfish, eccentric, opinionated, and tend to be loners. Marriage prospects and compatibility in relationships are based on zodiac matching. The best marriage for a rooster should be someone born in the years of the dragon, snake, or ox. Those born in years of the tiger, horse, sheep, monkey, and boar are the next best matches. Roosters are incompatible with other roosters and those born in years of the rat and dog. The worst match of all for a rooster is a rabbit.

Based on a countrywide survey conducted around 1980, twenty-seven breeds of chickens are popular in China. The Black Jiuyan, Chahua, Huiyuang Bearded, Jingyuan, Lindian, New Yangzhou, Putong, and Wuding are little known outside the country. However, the Langshan, the Silkie, and the famous Cochin are popular throughout the world.

It is interesting that in Latin, *Gallus* is the word for both "France" and "cock," because the *coq* has a long history as a symbol of France. In the thirteenth century, it was decreed that all churches should have the figure of a cock on their spires as a protector, the rooster being a symbol of vigilance, a trumpeter of a new day, a symbol of Christ, and a call to morning prayer. Later, the *Coq Galois* became the national emblem of France. Some claim the French adopted the cock as their national symbol as early as the fifteenth century. Others assert that it was not until after the 1789 revolution, when the cock began to appear on the French flag, that it became official. An engraving of the *coq* is proudly displayed on the French Constitution of 1791. It is also claimed that the rooster became an official symbol under the July Monarchy, when the bird adorned the top of the pole of the French flag in 1830. Regardless of when it became an official national symbol, the courage of the fighting cock was always an ideal image for French war propaganda. Its likeness is often engraved on war memorials. The pride of a national cuisine, the *poulet* often appears in French painting, sculpture, and porcelain, as well as in songs and literature. Statues of chickens are seen throughout the French countryside. Even the athletic clothing of the Federation Francaise d'Athletisme sports an image of the *coq*.

A resort on the French Riviera, Saint Tropez is well known today for its nude beaches and beautiful people. In 1055, it was called Ecclesia Sancti Torpetis, named after Torpetis, one of Nero's centurions who turned to Christianity and, as a result, was beheaded in A.D. 68. According to legend, Torpetis's body and head were placed in a boat and set adrift with a dog and a rooster. It was fully expected that the critters would get hungry and devour the man's remains. But after nineteen days at sea, the body was still intact when the boat came ashore where the town of Saint Tropez stands today. Two neighboring villages, Cogolin (meaning "small rooster" in old French) and Grimaud (meaning "dog" in old French) reinforce the legend.

In the ancient Jewish tradition, the cock was almost universally accepted as a substitute for the word "man." In fact, the Hebrew word for cock, *gever,* also means "man." At the Kapparah, a symbolic ceremony held on the eve of Yom Kippur, atonement offerings included killing a cock or hen and passing its body around the head of a sinner while saying, "This fowl is my substitute, this is my surrogate, this is my atonement. This cock (hen) goes to its death that I may enter into a long and happy life and into peace."

The cock and the hen were part of Jewish bridal processions. For some Orthodox Jews, on the day of Kapparah, the Day of Atonement, men sacrifice cocks and women sacrifice hens, so the person can enter a long and healthy life. It was believed that a crowing cock could drive away demons, and the image of a cock on amulets was a potent device against the evil eye. Another belief was that if a cock upset a vessel it should be killed immediately because evil spirits had seized it. To produce rain, one was to kill a white cock; tear out its entrails; mix them with various foods, spices, and wine; then hold them up to the sun and recite an incantation. Among Russian Jews, it was bad luck to leave a grave empty overnight. If a burial could not take place until the next day, a cock was partially buried as a substitute for the body.

The cock's crow has a powerful Christian significance. The most famous cock association is with St. Peter. During the Last

The cock represents the sunset in China. The red cock is the original form of the sun and protects against fire. The white cock protects against ghosts. A cock with a hen in a garden indicates the pleasures of rural life. In some Chinese initiation ceremonies, a white cock is killed to signify the death of the old life and the purity of the new. The Chinese word for *cock* sounds like the Chinese word for *fortunate,* which is why the rooster is used in funerary rites to ward off the powers of evil spirits.

In the year 2000, the Canadian government used "chicken sentinels" as an early warning system against any northbound birds or mosquitoes carrying the fatal West Nile virus from the United States. About six hundred hens were placed in special cages along the Canadian-U.S. border from Maine to Montana and were tested weekly for the dreaded disease. Luckily for the chickens, if bitten, they do not contract the disease.

Supper, Jesus told Peter—who had just pledged his unfaltering loyalty—"Verily, verily, I say unto thee, the cock shall not crow till thou hast denied me thrice" (John 13:38, cf. Matthew 26:34, Mark 14:30, Luke 22:34). After Jesus' arrest, when confronted, Peter panicked and protested any association with Christ. Upon Peter's first denial, "the cock crew" (Mark 14:68). Peter denied knowing Jesus two more times. Then, remembering what Jesus had said to him, he wept and repented (Mark 14:72). He later went on to become the leader of the Apostles and a martyr for the Christian faith. As a result, a depiction of a cock is often carved or painted with that of St. Peter. This association also makes the rooster one of the emblems of Christ's suffering and crucifixion.

Early Christians believed that the cock greeting the dawn represents Christ putting to flight the powers of evils and darkness. Like the rooster watching vigilantly for the coming of the sun, Christians were to watch for the second coming of Christ. The rooster also represented preachers to the faithful. Cocks fighting symbolized Christians striving for Christ, and carved roosters were often portrayed on the top of church columns. The gilded, solar cock guarded the steeples of churches through the hours of darkness when the bells are silent. As a weathervane, the rooster turns in all directions to watch for powers of evil.

In the Afro-Caribbean religion of Santeria, the chicken is sacrificed to feed the Orishas, spiritual entities associated with Christian saints. The birds are also used in rituals and secret rites. For example, to break the spell of a bewitched person, a live rooster is rubbed over the body of the bedeviled. Then that person is tied from head to toe with rope, which is immediately cut to "free" the enchanted person.

Chickens are sacrificed at feasts for the *loa*, the Voodun gods, in what is considered a benevolent, symbolic, and loving ritual. The selection of the proper chicken is important. A very thin bird would be an insult to the *loa*. The choice of color and sex of the chicken is determined by which *loa* it is to honor. For example, a chicken for Legba is white, for Loco yellow, and for Ghede black. The Hougan, or priest, holds a chicken by the legs and passes it over a kneeling crowd, an act that serves to empower the people and extract any evil from them. Then the chicken is "aired out" by being swung in the air in a practice called *ventailler*. The bird is offered food, and after it eats, it is sacrificed. Afterward, a plate is placed on the dead chicken to receive money for the cook or the *loa*, and those who contribute kneel or kiss the ground beside the chicken. Finally, the chicken is taken to be cleaned and cooked. Some of the meat is put on a special plate for the *loa* and set on the altar.

Why are chickens used in these ceremonies? My theory combines spirituality and practicality. In many cultures, birds symbolize a link to the Other World, the spiritual sphere. Some cultures believe that souls of the dying entered birds, which then flew off to heaven. Although chickens don't fly, the chicken is an available bird, one that is prolific and easy to breed. Consider the challenge if a black bird is required for a

Le Coq political

The cock was a powerful symbol during both world wars. This 1915 postcard (left) urges the French to turn in their gold in exchange for paper money to help the war effort. This 1945 postcard (below), designed by Paul Colins (1892–1986), a famous French poster artist, show the Coq Gaulois *crowing triumphantly over the defeat of the Germans.*

The cock and St. Peter

A cock looks up at St. Peter in this statue, found at the Living Cathedral of St. John the Divine in New York City. (Photograph by Martin Hintz)

"O Jerusalem. O Jerusalem, thou that killest the prophets and stonest them which are sent unto thee! How often would I have gathered thy children together, even as a hen gathereth her chickens under her wings—and ye would not!"

—Matthew 23:37; cf. Luke 13:34 (KJV)

ceremony. Wouldn't it be easier to use a domesticated black chicken than, for example, to try to catch a crow? I rest my case.

The Gnostic tradition, a mysterious, pre-Christian philosophical and religious movement dedicated to the pursuit of spiritual secrets, included a powerful, sun-related deity called Abraxas. Abraxas has the head of a rooster and two serpents for legs, representing God and the devil, as well as other apparent opposites, rolled into one.

In Buddhism, the cock, along with the pig and snake, is at the center of the Wheel of Life in Buddhist art. The Wheel is a map that, if followed, leads to salvation. The cock is a symbol of carnal passion and pride; the snake, aversion; and the pig, ignorance.

In ancient Celtic religions, cocks were used as sacrificial animals. During the pagan mid-winter festival called Imbolc (February 1 or 2), cocks were sacrificed by being buried alive.

Eating chicken is often forbidden by Hindu law.

In Scandinavian mythology, the rooster is the bird of the underworld, and its crowing wakes the heroes of Valhalla for the last great battle.

Nergal was a Sumerian deity sometimes depicted as a cock-headed god.

The rooster was the Egyptian hieroglyph of victory, and a rooster was often sacrificed when the Egyptian army attacked an enemy. Additionally, roosters were sacrificed to Osiris, the god of the dead and had an erotic association with the Egyptian Hermes (Thoth).

Easter eggs

The egg has long been the universal symbol of Easter. Before it was adopted by the Christians, the egg was honored by the ancient Greeks, Romans, Chinese, Egyptians, Persians, and Gauls in many pagan spring festivals as a symbol of birth and renewal after the long winter. In Christianity, the eggshell became a symbol of Christ's tomb and the egg a symbol of the rebirth of man. Easter cards, such as these vintage postcards, often portray chickens, chicks, and eggs.

Ludlow del.

Chapter 3

The Artful Chicken

The first recorded piece of chicken art dates back to prehistoric times. In Harappa, a great city in the valley of the Indus River in what is today Pakistan and one of the earliest (c. 3000 B.C.) agricultural civilizations, two clay figurines of a cock and a hen were found by archaeologists. This important find not only proved the existence of the chicken, but it also signified the beginning of an art that was to survive wars, depressions, and disease; an art that reflects the history and culture of civilization; an art that has finally been recognized as a legitimate genre—chicken art.

There aren't too many artistic "-isms" in which the chicken isn't. From realism to naturalism, impressionism to cubism, dadaism to surrealism, the chicken has inspired the masters, and a surprising number of great artists have pieces of chicken art in their body of work.

Facing page:
A chicken portrait
A renowned chicken artist, J. W. Ludlow often set the standard for the ideal chicken with his meticulous renderings.

Inset:
Chunky chicken
Using warmth and humor, artist Todd Warner strives to bridge the gap between animals and humans. The bodies of his animals are less than an inch thick, the legs are steel reinforced, the feet and head are clay. His tall, flat, skinny creatures are "a metaphor of the state of environment where animals are being pushed aside for technology." (Chicken Weathervane *artwork and photograph © 1993 Todd Warner Studio, Boca Raton, Florida, All Rights Reserved)*

English Archbishop Peckham (?–1279) considered non-preaching bishops to be "cocks which neither crow nor generate."

Classic Chickens of Ancient Greece and Rome

With the significant role that the chicken played in ancient Greece and Rome, it would stand to reason that chickens would be represented in their art. Unfortunately, most of the paintings on the walls of temples and houses no longer exist. Luckily, the beauty of Greek painting has survived on painted pottery, including vases, cups, amphoras, alabastrons, and other types of vessels. Chicken subject matter ranged from images of cockfighting; fully armed Athenians with cocks; boys riding cocks; cocks with Zeus, Hermes, Athena, and other gods; or just beautiful decorative cocks, usually in pairs, standing upright, proud, and bold. Statues of chickens on Greek and Roman sarcophagi portrayed cocks being fed, carried, and stroked. There are even references of pet cocks being buried with elaborate tombstones.

The story of Zeus and Ganymede was often captured in Greek art. Ganymede was the young, beautiful Trojan prince who Zeus fell in love with when he spotted the boy herding a flock on Mount Ida. A torrid love affair ensued. In the famous terra-cotta statue of Zeus and Ganymede at the Olympia Archeological Museum, Ganymede is holding a cock. A vase portrays the same theme—Ganymede, running at full speed, once again holding a cock, and being pursued by Zeus.

During the Roman era we find chicken art of a more utilitarian nature, with chickens adorning coins, lamps, intaglios, and ring stones.

Muse of the Masters: Chickens in European Art

After the fall of Rome, chicken art seems to have disappeared for more than a dozen centuries. We do find scattered images of chickens in European bestiaries as early as the twelfth century, but it was not until the end of the Middle Ages that chickens started popping up in art all over Europe.

Albrecht Dürer (1471–1528), a prolific and versatile Nuremberg artist, addressed chicken folklore in his art. His work spanned many mediums, including engravings, woodcuts, oil paintings, watercolors, drawings, and even altar pieces. Dürer was also known for his elaborate renderings of coats of arms. In one amusing example, a somewhat vexed-looking cock is standing atop a helmet, while below him is a rather frightened-looking lion. This image alluded to the legend that the lion, the most ferocious of all animals, feared the white cock more than anything. A sixteenth-century French proverb translates, "The lion trembles only at the cock's crow."

The chicken was ubiquitous in Dutch art beginning in the fifteenth century. In some paintings, the chickens are easy to spot; others are more difficult to discern. I

Right:
"Lead us not into temptation"
This humorous illustration by Albrecht Dürer shows an innocent-looking fox sweetly serenading a group of chickens. The allegorical drawing appeared next to the Lord's Prayer in a 1513 book of hours. The fox represents the devil attempting to lead the chickens—Christians—into temptation.

Facing page:
Chickens in the courtyard
Jan Steen's wit and humor are revealed in this delightful 1660 rendering of an idyllic sanctuary, filled with fowl. Titled The Poultry Yard, *it contrasts the sweetness and innocence of a young girl with the questionable characters of two men.*

searched for quite a while to find a chicken in the paintings of Hieronymus Bosch (1450–1516). In his strange paintings, Bosch depicted weird people, ugly demons, distorted animals, unidentifiable objects, and even odd foodstuff. I was unable to find even a trace of a chicken in his work until one day I discovered the book *A Bestiary for Saint Jerome: Animal Symbolism in European Religious Art*. In the bestiary under "cock" was the statement: "Aside from a single painting, *Saint Jerome in Penitence* by Hieronymus Bosch in Ghent, the cock has not been found in the Jerome context." My adrenaline soared with anticipation, but it waned just as quickly when, upon careful scrutiny, I could not find a single cock in the painting. I reread the bestiary and was relieved to read that the multitude of fauna and flora in the painting were obscure and could easily go unnoticed. I finally found the chicken lurking in the shadows at the very bottom of the painting, vulnerably close to a curled-up sleeping fox.

There is even a chicken, albeit a mysterious one, in Rembrandt Harmenszoon van Rijn's (1606–1669) most famous painting *Night Watch* (1642). Originally titled *The Militia Company of Captain Frans Banning Cocq, Night Watch* depicts a scene of city guardsmen awaiting orders. In the center of the painting, bathed in light, is a little girl with a white chicken hanging at her waist. The exact interpretation of the girl and chicken is left to speculation. Some say it is the ghost-like image of Rembrandt's late wife, Saskia, who had died that year. Others identify her as the Queen of Sports with a game bird hanging at her waist. Whatever the explanation, this painting shows the chicken did not go unnoticed by Rembrandt, unquestionably the most famous of the seventeenth-century Dutch painters and one of the most famous painters of all time.

In the later part of the seventeenth century, the Dutch naturalists loved to incorporate a subliminal context into their work, and the chicken represented a variety of symbols, often of a sexual nature. Gerald Dou (1613–1675) painted erotic symbols into *Woman Holding a Cock at the Window*. The symbols are the woman holding a dead cock, often considered a sexual image, plus a metal bucket and an open vessel that has fallen on its side, both of which are perhaps symbols of a female nature. Also depicted is a snuffed-out candle, which has phallic overtones. The meaning of the empty birdcage in the painting is open for discussion.

Another Dutch artist, J. van Horst, allegedly depicts a symbolic copulation in his painting *Market Scene* (1596). It shows a wicker basket full of poultry, a man holding a hen, and a basket full of eggs. Pieter Aertsen painted chickens and other animal flesh in abundance in *Butcher Shop with the Flight into Egypt* (1561). In the foreground, a butcher shop is overfilled with dead meats, including chickens, and Mary is seen offering alms to the poor in the distance, depicting an interesting contrast between the worlds of the material and the spiritual.

Dutch painter Jan Steen (1626–1679) is well known for his droll paintings depicting everyday life in Holland. His paintings are theatrical, telling a story with a slight grin, and his characters are entertaining, even ludicrous at times. In *The Poultry Yard*, Steen portrays ten-year-old Jacoba Maria van Wasenauer, innocently offering milk to a lamb. She is surrounded by exotic fowl and gazed upon by two lecherous yet (seemingly) harmless male visitors.

Melchoir de Hondekoeter (also spelled Hondecoeter, 1636–1695) was a prolific

"She's no spring chicken;
she's on the wrong side of thirty,
if she be a day."
—Jonathan Swift (1667–1745)

Facing page:
Want to see my chicken etchings?
Melchoir de Hondekoeter, better known for his dazzling skills in painting exotic and colorful plumage, also etched dramatic fowl.

Portrait of a Chicken Artist: Pablo Picasso

Pablo Picasso (1881–1973) was a prolific artist. But more impressive was the fact that he was a prolific chicken artist. Throughout his lengthy career (1896 to 1955), chickens—mostly cocks—appear often as powerful, significant symbols in his works. With the possible exception of horses and bulls, roosters are the most important animal representations in his works. They are important not only as icons, but also as reflections of Picasso's emotional state and personal life.

Picasso started sketching charcoal and chalk cocks in 1896, at the age of fifteen. He continued to draw cock doodles of minor significance until 1921, when he painted his first major cock oil, *Dog and Cock*. Scholars label the painting as being part of his synthetic cubist period. He then moved away from synthetic cubism, also putting the cock aside for eleven years. Then, in 1932, he sculpted *Cock,* an elegant and graceful bronze of a strutting rooster, one that is proud, regal, and powerful.

***The Cock of the Liberation* (*Le Coq de la Liberation*), 1944**
Picasso painted and sculpted many chickens, mostly cocks and an occasional hen, throughout his lengthy and prolific artistic career. Painted while Picasso was living in occupied Paris, The Cock of the Liberation *reveals his anti-Nazi sentiments,* le coq gauloise *being a national symbol of France. (Oil on canvas; 39½" x 31¾", Milwaukee Art Museum, Gift of Mrs. Harry Lynde Bradley, M1959.372, © 2002 Estate of Pablo Picasso/Artists Rights Society [ARS], New York)*

Girl with Cock (1938) is probably the most telling of Picasso's cock paintings. At the time of the painting, the artist's life was in chaos, stemming from ongoing marital problems with Olga, his wife; the tension between his two mistresses (Mary-Therese Walter and Dora Maar); a civil war in his Spanish homeland; and the onset of World War II. Undoubtedly, these factors contributed to the disturbing subject matter. *Girl with Cock* portrays a cold, strange, androgynous-looking person—which some critics claim resembles Picasso—holding on her lap a terrified cock by the throat. The poor, helpless cock is controlled, held on his back in a submissive position and about to be sacrificed or castrated.

Picasso said that the painting represented the destruction of a helpless humanity by the forces of evil, meaning the sacrifice of the innocent. This metaphor may be true on one level, but knowing of Picasso's preoccupation with sex, it is fascinating to interpret the painting on a subconscious or Freudian level. If the girl represents Picasso and the cock is a phallic symbol, did Picasso feel his masculinity was threatened? Did he possibly feel a bit of a castration complex? Or, does the girl symbolize the three women in Picasso's life, and the cock represent Picasso himself—

an interesting statement of vulnerability and a feeling of submission?

Two other paintings painted the same year reinforced Picasso's seemingly threatened sense of masculinity. Both are entitled *Cock*, and each portrays a screeching, fearful, nonmasculine rooster.

"Cocks, there have always been cocks, but like everything else in life, we have to discover them, just like Corot discovered the morning and Renoir young girls," Picasso said. "Cocks have always been seen, but never as well as in American weather vanes."

While living in occupied France during World War II, Picasso painted and sculpted numerous apolitical cocks. Having no sympathy for the Nazis, he was closely watched and forced to refrain from any controversy. Perhaps the cocks of this period, including one entitled *Cock of the Liberation* (1944) were merely symbols of French support, the cock having long been a symbol of the French spirit.

In *Cock and Knife* (1947), the cock is once again being sacrificed, his feet bound and his neck slit, as he lies on what appears to be an altar. In 1953, in another of Picasso's works, a poor, helpless cock is ripped apart by a female cat. Why is it not surprising that Picasso had just been jilted by Francoise Gilot? In 1955, Picasso came full circle with the symbolic cock, as he painted his last rooster figure—one filled with strength and dignity and protecting a gentle, peaceful female dove. Although Picasso's personal life always seemed to be chaotic, the painting appears to reflect a time of complacency and comfort.

Dutch artist of exotic fowl, including chickens. His realistic style of painting and etching showed off his masterful ability to create lush detail. His paintings have a dreamlike quality, and often the underlying message reveals the contrast between an idyllic world and uncivilized behavior, with the chickens in his paintings symbolizing humans at their behavioral worst. An exception is *A Cock, Hens and Chicks* (c. 1668), in which Hondekoeter paints a chicken world in a more peaceful state.

In his writings, Saint Augustine (A.D. 354–430) describes the Christian church as "A hen with chicks. She not only keeps them warm, but also loves as her own the chicks of whatever other bird she may have hatched, so the church yearns to call not only her Christians but others, whether Gentiles or Jews. . . ." Flemish painter Frans Floris (1516–1570) reflects this metaphor in *The Winged Christ* with a hen and her chicks standing guard at the feet of the crucified Christ.

William Hogarth (1697–1764) was a leading English artist in the first half of the eighteenth century. He rejected the formal, stiff, and grandiose style that dominated art after the Middle Ages and introduced humor from everyday life—including low-life—into his art. Subjects as diverse as prostitution, debauchery, and infidelity are portrayed in his works.

Hogarth's painting entitled *Pit-Ticket Cockfight* is an accurate depiction of the strange mix of characters in the bedlamlike atmosphere of a cockfight. The delightful and humorous picture shows the seamier side of life—fighting, gambling, drunkenness—with very little attention being paid to the cocks. It shows Lord Albemarle Bertie, who, although blind, is said to have been

"They are sorry houses where the hens crow and the cock holds his peace."
—John Florio (1553?–1625)

"If I didn't start painting, I would have raised chickens."
—Grandma Moses (Anna Mary Robertson Moses, 1860–1961)

Henri de Toulouse-Lautrec (1864–1901), best known for his portraits and his scenes of Paris, created a bestiary called *Histoires Naturelles*, with text by Jules Renard. In *Histoires Naturelles*, both hens and roosters are eloquently depicted—verbally by Renard and artistically by Toulouse-Lautrec's simple, impressionistic style.

addicted to cocking. A thief is trying to extract a bank note from him. On the wall hangs a portrait of Nan Rawlings, also known as Deptford Nan or the Duchess of Deptford, who was a well-known "cock-feeder" or trainer at that time. A deaf parson is being yelled at through a megaphone. The strange shadow is a defaulter, who has not paid his betting losses and who had been drawn up to the ceiling in a basket, as required by cockpit law. He is offering his watch in payment.

Sir Joshua Reynolds (1723–1792) was one of England's most notable portrait painters and helped form the Royal Academy of Arts in 1768. He was the most fashionable painter of his day, producing portraits of the wealthy, including charming portraits of children. He became the academy's first president in 1784 and was appointed painter to the king. Lady Catherine Pelham Clinton, the subject of Reynolds's painting by the same name, was the only daughter of Henry Pelham Clinton, the Earl of Lincoln, and the granddaughter of Henry, Duke of Newcastle. The portrait shows the young girl holding her apron full of seed with one hand, while with the other hand she scatters the seed to eager chickens.

Toward the end of his life, leading Spanish artist Francisco de Goya (1746–1828) was encumbered by the onset of deafness and disillusioned by Napoleon's invasion and occupation of Spain from 1808 to 1813. During this period, Goya painted numerous pictures of slaughtered fowl, including one entitled *Still Life*, which is the image of a very lifeless, defeated, and dramatically dead chicken. Perhaps this recurring image is a symbol of human beings' inhumanity, or perhaps it is a self-reflection of Goya's own enfeebled state.

With the French fascination with the *poulet*, it would stand to reason that the chicken would be prevalent in French art, perhaps the rooster more than the hen.

Return from the Market by French artist Jean Baptiste Simeon Chardin (1699–1779) infuses domesticity with dignity by depicting a peasant woman holding a sack with a dead chicken in it. The woman exudes an attitude of contentment, and the dead chicken also seems at peace in its expired state. This chicken appears to be nothing more that what it is—a dead chicken. It is neither a metaphor nor an exotic idealized rendering of fancy fowl. Instead, it is simply a typical dead chicken that will be served at a typically delicious French meal.

Jean Ignace Isidore Gerard, better known as J. J. Grandville (1803–1847), was a popular French illustrator, cartoonist, and political satirist. He illustrated such notable works as La Fontaine's *Fables, Gulliver's Travels* by Jonathan Swift, and *The Adventures of Robinson Crusoe* by Daniel Defoe. His trademark was fusing animal heads onto human bodies, and roosters and hens were an important part of his menagerie. He first gained public acclaim in Paris with his *Les Métamorphoses du Jour*, a book with seventy-one designs of animal/humans, each with an accompanying message. His anthropomorphisms are used to point out the vices and follies of people.

Charles Jacque (1813–1894) began his artistic career in Paris as a graphic artist and illustrator, but his heart belonged in the country. In 1848, he moved to Barbizon, a village on the outskirts of the forest of Fontainebleau, southeast of Paris, in search of rustic bliss. While in Barbizon, he became a chicken farmer and breeder, writing a book, *Le Poulailler*, that recorded his chicken experiences. In one very beautiful

painting, Jacque infused his chickens with light, sensuous textures, and a seeming randomness of action in an informal setting.

In mid-nineteenth-century England, the poultry world was documented with beautiful renderings of chicken breeds. In fact, some were so realistic, they were used to standardize the breeds and serve as guidelines for judges.

J. W. Ludlow (1840–1916) was one of the major artists of this period. His greatest chicken paintings were fifty meticulous renderings of perfect chickens in Lewis Wright's *The Illustrated Book of Poultry*. His chickens were majestic, all in formal poses, with fine details of feather patterns. Ludlow also illustrated *Cassell's Poultry Book,* another chicken classic. Incidentally, Wright (1838–1905) was also the author of *The Book of Poultry* and *The Practical Poultry Keeper*. At the age of nine, he started raising Minorcas and later moved over to Brahmas. His poultry authority brought him fame and fortune.

This Victorian period became a great era of illustrated magazines, as the art of illustration came into its own. Harrison William Weir (1824–1906) was a well-known animal painter, illustrator, and author. He drew for the *Illustrated London News*; illustrated numerous poultry books, including *The Poultry Book* by W. B. Tegetmeire; and wrote *Our Poultry*, which boasts of being one of the most profusely illustrated poultry books ever published. Weir also raised and exhibited poultry.

Chicken heads up

French illustrator J. J. Grandville is noted for his animal-headed humans. Plate 32 in Les Metamorphoses du Jour *tells of unhappily married French men: "To sell a wife in England / Is it done, as they often say? / I believe it is for so many French husbands / Would even pay for their good riddance."*

Portrait of a Chicken Artist: Marc Chagall

The paintings of Marc Chagall (1887–1985) exude joy, hope, and love. His deep love of his Russian homeland, his Jewish heritage, and his family are ever present in his works. Chagall had a fervent love for animals, including chickens, and he felt that art must harmonize with nature.

In Chagall's paintings, the rooster appears again and again and again. As a guardian, the bird protects lovers under his wing. He gently leads a bride and groom from the Eiffel Tower to their wedding. Half-cock, half-horse, a rooster pulls a child through the air on a sled. He wraps himself protectively around a child. He carries a child on his back, playing a pipe. Chagall fuses cocks with nature, women, flowers, trees, actors, and musicians. His roosters often seem like angels.

Chagall's love and sympathy for animals may stem from his grandfather's profession as a butcher. In his autobiography, *My Life,* Chagall reveals that the slaughter of animals left a deep impression on him as a young boy. He saw humans as implacable killers of their fellow beings, the beasts. He considered animals so akin to humans "that we are stirred to the depths of our being." He felt that comparing people and animals in his paintings wasn't accidental or just an aesthetic or pictorial need.

Chagall's pure and innocent animals seem amazed that humans can be so cruel. His roosters are often red, the color of sacrifice. The chickens in his work have eyes filled with tenderness, love, suffering, innocence, nostalgia, and a hint of joy. Chagall's chickens are profound, revealing a man who deeply cared about life.

Chicken as self

Chickens feature prominently in many Chagall works, including his Self-Portrait (1959–1968). *(Scala/Art Resource, NY, © 2002 Artists Rights Society [ARS], New York/ADAGP, Paris)*

Chicken art in the Victorian period reflected a public that wanted provincial art, pictures with a story, often with a moral, and a big dose of sentimentality. Chickens in idyllic settings and romantic renderings of barnyard bliss were the style during this era. Among the many Victorian painters to include chickens in their work were Edgar Hunt (1876–1955), William Huggins (1820–1884), William Baptiste Baird (1847–1899), H. C. Bryant (1860–1884), and John W. Wood (1839–1886).

In the summer of 1874, a momentous occasion happened in the history of chicken art. Two great impressionist painters, Pierre Auguste Renoir and Edouard Manet, painted the family of fellow artist Claude Monet. The historic painting sessions took place at the summer homes of Manet and Monet. While Manet painted the Monet family, Renoir painted beside Manet, and Monet worked nearby.

In both paintings, Madame Monet is formally attired, complete with hat, full skirt, and fan, while she sits on the lawn with her son affectionately by her side. More important is the fact that in each painting, beautiful impressionistic chickens are present. Rather than imitate the exactness of a chicken, these impressionists diffused them with light, giving them a soft and airy tonality. They placed their subjects in a natural setting, as a part of an idyllic scene. In each of their renditions, the chicken is a regal bystander, an observer of rural life.

John Heartfield (1891–1968) was part of the Berlin dada group, which, like other dadaists, felt the need to attack and disrupt the staid morality and the cheap sentimentality of the bourgeois. Members of the group were anti-war and anti-establishment, and because art was clearly part of the bour-

Rural chicken bliss

At the age of thirty-five, Charles Jacque, a well-known Parisian painter, moved to the country in search of rustic bliss. He found it by raising and painting chickens. Jacque eventually became one of the foremost painters of animals, including chickens. Une Basse-cour *(1860s) depicts realistically rendered chickens hunting for grain. (Reprinted with permission of the Musée des Beaux-Arts de Béziers)*

Faberge Eggs

Peter Carl Faberge (1846–1920), businessman and jeweler extraordinaire, created the House of Faberge in Saint Petersburg in 1870. It thrived until the revolution in 1917. Inspired by the egg, the House of Faberge created the ultimate in extravagant design—the famous Imperial Eggs.

When Nicholas II came to the throne in 1894, he commissioned Faberge to create presents for his wife, Alexandra, and his mother, Maria. Thus began the annual "egg surprise" and from 1895 until the fateful year 1917, fifty-two eggs were presented to the two czarinas. A total of fifty-four eggs were made, but those made in 1917 were never delivered.

Though most are just extravagant eggs, some bear the image of hens and roosters. In 1903, the House of Faberge created the Chanticleer Egg. On the hour, Chanticleer, made of gold with yellow, blue, and green enamel and adorned with rose diamonds, springs from the top of the egg, nods his head, flaps his wings, and moves his beak as if to crow.

Chanticleer Egg
The Faberge Chanticleer Egg (1903) is now part of the Forbes Magazine Collection in New York City. (Photograph by the Forbes Magazine Collection, New York © All Rights Reserved)

geois world, they were also anti-art. Heartfield, born Helmut Herzfelde, had chutzpah in the face of the strident German militarism of his day. He changed his name to protest the kaiser's insistence that patriotic Germans greet each other with "God punish England." This independence later translated into art that was political, aggressive, humorous, and acidic. Heartfield is credited as one of the originators of an artistic technique called photomontage, which he developed into a powerful art form. In *Now Don't Be Scared—He's a Vegetarian* (1936), also titled *Have no Fear—He's a Vegetarian,* Heartfield created a comical metaphor to mock the enemy. This poignant image portrays Hitler, with a sinister leer, sharpening his knives while an innocent French chicken awaits its fate.

Rene Magritte (1898–1967), a surrealist painter living in France and Belgium, painted *Variante de la Tristesse* (*Variation of Sadness*) in 1957. The painting depicts a chicken contemplating an egg in a cup. Other notable surrealist chicken paintings include Joan Miro's *The Farm* (1920) and *Tilled Field* (1921–1922), and *Ibdes D'Aragon* (1935) by Andre Masson.

American Chicken Art

Early European settlers in North America were more concerned with pragmatic issues—food, shelter, and clothing—than with chicken art. In fact, art in general was frowned upon as irreverent and self-indulgent. The Puritan work ethic allowed little time for pleasure. This attitude is summed up by an anonymous Boston writer:

> The Plowman that raiseth Grain is more serviceable to Mankind, than the Painter who draw only to please

the eye. The hungry man would count fine Pictures, but a mean entertainment. The Carpenter who builds a good House to defend us from the Wind and Weather, is more serviceable that the curious Carver, who employs his Art to Please his fancy. This condemns not Painting, or Carving, but only shows that what's more substantially serviceable to Mankind, is much preferable to what is less necessary.

Early American artists suffered from a feeling of inferiority to their European counterparts and, in general, felt a lack of identity in the world of art. They often turned to Europe for guidance, which resulted in "masterpieces" in the European tradition—realistic portraits and historical, religious, and mythological paintings done on pompous and grandiose scales.

However, several American artists were oblivious to the European scene and became known as folk artists. Although definitions are risky, "folk art" implies that the

Farmyard Fowls

John James Audubon (1785–1851), American artist extraordinaire, produced thousands of bird paintings. Farmyard Fowls *is one of only a handful that feature chickens as their subject. (Gift of E. J. L. Hallstrom, photograph © 2002 Board of Trustees, National Gallery of Art, Washington, D.C.)*

artist is self-taught, with little or no formal training about the principles of art, lighting, and form. Their work is not executed in the traditionally realistic style and is produced outside the mainstream of fashion. Folk art was both artistic and practical. And in American folk art, chickens were a great source of inspiration.

As the country expanded and settlers developed new areas, hard-working itinerant artists called limners roamed from town to town painting portraits. A new feeling of the importance of the "common man" was emerging in this country, and many wanted to preserve a family likeness for posterity. Although most art from this period is unsigned and folk art was seldom associated with particular artists, in a few instances, artists with a recognizable style emerged.

Jacob Maentel (1763–1863) was one of the many limners who traveled the countryside. Unlike other professional folk artists, Maentel used watercolor for full-length portraits of Pennsylvania-German farmers, their wives, and children. His painting *Boy with Rooster* (1815) is an amusing watercolor and ink. The boy's profile resembles that of his pet cock, and Maentel mirrors the

Savory Sunday supper
William Harnett (1848–1892) was a trompe d'oeil *("trick of the eye") still-life painter who was devoted to the exact replication of life. He was also very nearsighted and painted his subjects the exact size at which he perceived them. In* For Sunday's Dinner, *each feather, each plucked follicle of a dead chicken is rendered with meticulous detail. Like other artists, he often couldn't afford a live model, so the subject regularly became his dinner. (Oil on canvas; 37⅛ x 21⅛ in., Wilson L. Mead Fund, 1958.296, reproduction © The Art Institute of Chicago, All Rights Reserved)*

youngster's hair in the rooster tail—which also appears to be a part of the boy.

Wilhelm Schimmel (1817–1890) was a woodcarver whose family came to America from Germany and settled in the Cumberland Valley of Pennsylvania. He wandered a twenty-mile range of the countryside carrying a basket of carvings, which he sold for ten cents or a quarter or in exchange for food, drink, or lodging. It is rumored that every tavern, restaurant, and bar in the region had at least one now-valuable Schimmel carving. Many of his carvings feature chickens as their subject.

After the colonies became the United States, the new quest for a national identity extended into the art world. While portraiture was still dominant, artists became interested in American landscapes and nature, as exemplified by the work of Winslow Homer, Ben Austrian, Mary Smith, Susan Waters, Arthur Tait, and others.

Winslow Homer (1836–1910) is regarded as one of the greatest of nineteenth-century American painters. Though he is best known for the seascapes of his later career, chickens do appear in his portfolio. Like so many American artists, Homer began as an illustrator, making many designs for wood engravings published in *Harper's Weekly*. By 1863, he had begun to paint and depicted many Civil War scenes. In 1867, he turned to celebrating old-fashioned rural values in a nation undergoing rapid change and urbanization. It was during this period that chickens appeared in his works, including *Barnyard with Boy Feeding Chickens* and *The Rooster*.

Mary Smith (1842–1878) relished country life, gardening, painting, and raising a large flock of poultry. Her passionate love of nature is evident in the meticulous

Like boy, like rooster

Maentel's Boy with Rooster *shows a clear example of pet-look-alike syndrome, a blessing (or an affliction) of people who begin to look like their pets.*

A mother hen's love

Ben Austrian loved chickens. Motherhood, *one of his many hen and chicks paintings, evokes his deep admiration for the hen and her protectiveness toward her young brood. In his book about his great uncle's life,* Ben Austrian: Artist, *Geoffrey Austrian says this loving tribute to the hen was based on Ben's deep feelings for his own mother. Austrian was partial to hens and chicks rather than roosters, and he painted the fairer of the sex with sentimentality. His relationship with chickens began when, as a young boy, he was sent to a farm near Reading, Pennsylvania, to cure a childhood illness. (Courtesy of the Reading Public Museum, Reading, Pennsylvania)* details of her paintings, including one entitled *Chickens and Squirrel*.

Susan C. Waters (1823–1900), another noted animal painter, received her artistic training as an itinerant portrait painter, traveling with her husband throughout southern New York and Pennsylvania. Influenced by the realistic style of European art, she became known for her depiction of farm creatures, including *Chickens*, which she painted in the 1870s.

Nicknamed "The Chick Painter of Berks County," self-taught painter Ben Austrian (1870–1921) of Reading, Pennsylvania, was influenced by the *trompe d'oeil* style of William Harnett. He painted chickens throughout his career, including one called *Hasn't Scratched Yet*. This work attracted the attention of the company that made Bon Ami cleaning products and was adapted to become the Bon Ami Chick logo. Austrian used his maulstick to hypnotize his chicken subjects, so they'd remain still while he painted them.

Arthur F. Tait (1819–1905) lived between New York City and the Adirondacks, painting sporting and wilderness scenes, from 1850 to 1888. His work for Currier and Ives gave him national recognition. In 1888, he gave up painting wild game animals and birds to concentrate on domestic animals and fowl. He painted upwards of 1,600 pictures, with chickens and domestic animals comprising about 30 percent of his work. Of these, chickens represent 37 percent, a figure that computes to about 178 paintings of chickens.

John Steuart Curry (1897–1946) found great beauty in nature, particularly in farm life, but he seemed to have varying opinions about chickens. In his sketches of animal studies, the rooster is portrayed as proud and noble, the hen plump and sweet. Yet in a painting called *The Tornado*, the chicken's intelligence seems to be in question. With the wind tunnel looming on the horizon, a sense of urgency and panic is felt by all—except for the chicken, who looks unaware and unconcerned. In *The Hen and the Hawk*, on the other hand, the hen is pictured in the supreme act of motherhood—defending her chicks from the fierce hawk. Though ill-equipped to fend off the attack, she shuts her eyes, flaps her wings, and even manages to get her plump body off the ground—a wonderful portrayal of motherly love.

George Luks (1867–1933) is part of the American Ashcan School, a group of artists who painted realistic and unidealized pictures of daily life. The group was based in New York City around 1908 to 1913. On one of my trips to New York in search of chickens, a high point was to be a visit to *Mrs. Gamely*, a painting by Luks housed at the Whitney Museum of American Art. It is a picture of the quintessential grandmother holding a chicken. Mrs. Gamely has a sweetness and serenity about her that makes me think of my grandmother, who died in a nursing home in 1996 at the age of 102. Unfortunately, I never met *Mrs. Gamely*. She was out of town—on loan to a museum in Detroit.

A. O. Schilling (1882–1958) is regarded as one of America's foremost chicken artists. A painter, illustrator, photographer, lecturer, writer, and poultry fancier, his work is ubiquitous in the world of chicken art. For many years he was the official artist for the *American Standard of Perfection* and the American Poultry Association. As an avid photographer, Schilling was quite adept at creating the ideal of a breed by retouching his photos. He had no qualms about chang-

"The hen is the wisest of all the animal creations because she never cackles until after the egg is laid."
—Abraham Lincoln (1809–1865), referring to General Joseph ("Fighting Joe") Hooker's overconfidence about beating the Confederate forces

Hooker's Army of the Potomac was eventually defeated by General Robert E. Lee at the Battle of Chancellorville (May 24, 1863), and Hooker was forced to resign his command.

"It is a no good hen that cackles in your house and lays in another's."
—Thomas Fuller (1654–1734), *Gnomologia*

ing the comb or the stance of a chicken to create the image of a perfect specimen.

Yasuo Kuniyoshi (1889–1953) did not set out to be an artist, let alone one who painted beautiful chickens. He was born in Okayama, Japan, and came alone to the United States in 1906 with a mere $200 dollars in his pocket, no contacts, and only a few words of English. Those challenges did not distract him from studying art for three years at night school while working menial jobs. He moved to New York in 1910 and by 1914 joined the Modernist Independent School and then the Art Students League, making friends with many artists. His beautiful rooster paintings reflect the Japanese reverence for the cock. In *Cock Calling the Dawn* (1923), Kuniyoshi's portrait of a regal rooster fills the canvas. The bird stands amidst beautiful greenery, and a faint hint of sunrise foretells the coming of the dawn.

Although some describe him as an urban modernistic folk artist, Milton Avery (1885–1965) is really in a class by himself. He is one of America's greatest colorists and depicted everyday life without extraneous detail, merely suggesting the essence of an idea. He was influenced by folk art, and although his works have a modern feel to them, they still remain traditional and American. His paintings reflect a simple, more natural world, where a gentle and charming humor is revealed. Avery's chickens evoke a sense of harmony and serenity. They seem innocent and untroubled by a modern world.

"The chicken is the country's, but the city eats it."
—George Herbert (1593–1633)

Painter, storyteller, and blues musician Jimmy Lee Sudduth (1910–) is acclaimed as one of Alabama's most popular folk artists. He is known as a "dirt" painter, because he uses real mud to create shades. He also blends natural dyes, such as turnip greens, with dirt, to produce bright and vibrant colors. A prolific animal painter, Sudduth empowers his animals with dignity, and they appear larger than life. I am the owner of a beautiful Sudduth painting, which hangs on my dining room wall (see the introduction). It portrays a poultry grande dame—a grandiose hen with a crimson body and hackles and a tail textured with other materials. She has a contented expression of maternal bliss, as her seven baby chickens scurry behind her.

Bill Traylor (1854–1947) was born into slavery on an Alabama plantation. After emancipation, Traylor continued to live on the plantation until 1938 when he moved to Montgomery. At the age of eighty-five, he started to draw and paint, drawing on whatever subjects he could find. His work was a visual remembrance from his rural days, with many drawings of animals. Between 1939 and 1942, he was said to have drawn more than 1,800 images. One of them is *Yellow Chicken*, a wonderful painting of a dancing chicken that exudes happiness.

Chaim Soutine (1893–1943) is labeled an expressionist painter, one who rejects the imitation of the outer world of reality for the expression of an inner world of feeling and imagination. He is also labeled the "painter of anguish." Soutine's inner feelings about chickens are certainly revealed in his work. He hated chickens so much that, from around 1924 to 1926, he painted more than twenty versions of dead birds that are all plucked and hanging on hooks. Unlike Harnett's peaceful dead chicken, Soutine's chickens all seem to have suffered an agonizing demise. One of Soutine's childhood punishments—being locked in the family's chicken coop—always haunted him. Painting dead chickens may have been a way for the artist to purge his childhood memories. His inner world of chicken loathing is especially evident in his *Dead Fowl.*

The *Odalisk* by Robert Rauschenberg (1925–) appears to be the ultimate modern rendering of the Bremen Town Musicians (see chapter 4)—a three-dimensional pyramid of inanimate objects with the cock on top. Some scholars claim the *Odalisk* actually portrays a French prostitute, *poule de luxe*, atop a totem collage. Rauschenberg, however, has suggested that art does not have rules, and he has raised questions about the conventional functions of the discipline. Thus, if Rauschenberg's objects have no symbolic value, nor are they autobiographical, perhaps then a chicken is just a chicken.

If bigger is better and more is more, contemporary American artist Douglas Argue's (1962–) untitled chicken painting is unarguably the ultimate chicken painting. Not only is it monumental—twelve by eighteen feet—but it also evokes a feeling of infinite chickens, each a unique entity with its own personality and details. He painted without models, yet each chicken is different. Argue worked for eighteen months to produce this chicken tour de force, this chicken coup de gras, this acme of chicken painting. He has never been around chickens and has no particular feelings about them. Although it depicts a large-scale chicken-raising operation, Argue protests that this painting is neither a social commentary about mass production nor the plight of chickens. A particular chicken company, though, did not interpret it that way when Argue asked them to buy it. They indignantly asserted, "Our chickens are all free range." For some reason, this painting

Modern folk chickens

White Chicken *(1947) is just one of Milton Avery's chicken paintings. His others include* Pink Rooster *(1943),* Canadian Chickens *(1948),* Chicken *(1948), and* Rooster Domain *(1948). He also produced a woodcut called* Rooster *(1953). His interest in chickens during the 1940s was perhaps inspired by his summer stays in Woodstock, New York, a rural farming area with an abundance of chickens. (All rights reserved, The Metropolitan Museum of Art, Gift of Joyce Blaffer von Bothmer, 1975. [1975.210] Photograph © 1980 The Metropolitan Museum of Art)*

Maximum chickens

At twelve by eighteen feet, Douglas Argue's untitled 1994 work is without a doubt the largest chicken painting in the history of art. Owned by Gerard Cafesjian, the painting can be seen in the Weisman Art Museum in Minneapolis, Minnesota. (Collection of Gerhard Cafesjian, on loan to the Weisman Art Museum; reprinted with permission of the artist)

Portrait of a Chicken Artist: Grant Wood

In the 1930s, American artists were turning to their own roots for inspiration instead of idealizing the art of Europe. This movement was called regionalism, and Grant Wood (1891–1942) was among its leading figures, along with John Steuart Curry, Thomas Hart Benton, and others.

A man after my own heart, Grant Wood loved chickens. His first drawing, which he drew at age three, showed a cluster of tiny arcs or half-moons, all positioned in the same direction. He told his mother that they were chickens. Proudly, she did see a resemblance between the abstract forms and the family's Plymouth Rocks. Throughout his career, Wood never tired of the birds. He drew crowing and fighting roosters, and hens in a variety of moods.

We see chickens in Wood's early works *Old Stone Barn* (1919) and *Feeding the Chickens* (1919). In *Dinner for Threshers* (1934), the viewer's eye—or at least the chicken lover's eye—is drawn to the hens outside the house. Hens also strut across the lawn in the *Birthplace of Herbert Hoover* (1931). Wood's sister Nan is holding a baby chicken in his favorite painting, one that he never parted with, called *Portrait of Nan* (1933).

Two of my favorite chicken paintings are Wood's *Appraisal* (1931) and *Adolescence* (1940). Both include meticulous renderings of chickens, combined with a comical and wry message.

Wood is a master of weaving a visual tale of humor and poignancy. *Appraisal* shows two contrasting women, one from the country, the other from the city. The healthy, handsome woman from the country wears unassuming clothes and holds a beautiful Plymouth Rock, while the fleshy, double-chinned, fur-clad woman from the city holds a purse. Reportedly, they are discussing the price of the hen. Grant's heart belonged in the country, so this allegory of labor verses leisure reveals his sentiments about the human condition in rural American society contrasting with that of urban life.

Wood first drew *Adolescence* in 1931 on brown wrapping paper. Later he made a trial lithograph of it, and finally in 1940, he redid the piece as an oil painting. This masterpiece is a poignant barnyard metaphor about the pain and awkwardness of growing up. The pubescent chicken with pinfeathers at the center of the painting is looking awkward, shy, and insecure as she modestly attempts to hide her body. She is crowded by two scowling authority figures—two matronly hens.

A story in Wood's biography tells how he became fond of the chick in Nan's portrait and kept it in his studio after that painting was finished. Later, a group of actors was using the studio and left behind a prop—a rubber cigarette—that the chicken mistakenly took for food. The poor fowl choked and died. Mrs. Wood, without a sentimental attachment to the bird, plucked and prepared the carcass for supper. The sad sight of this plucked chicken was said to have inspired *Adolescence*.

D'Anvers Belgian Quail

This painting of the D'Anvers Belgian Quail breed is by Diane Jacky, today's most prolific chicken artist. Hundreds of her realistically rendered oil paintings appear in the American Standard of Perfection, *setting the standard for the ideal of the breed. She has been painting chickens for more than thirty years, and her paintings adorn the walls of chicken art collectors all over the world. (Artwork © Diane Jacky)* hits a raw nerve in the poultry industry.

Milwaukee, Wisconsin, artist Eugene Vow Bruenchenhein (1910–1983) wore many "hats," describing himself as a "Freelance Artist, Poet and Sculptor, Innovator, Arrow maker and Plant Man, Bone Artifacts Constructor, Photographer and Architect, Philosopher." He certainly was an eccentric and ingenious in his use of delicate chicken bones to construct tiny chairs, intricate little thrones, and complex bone towers.

Conceptual/performing artist Jeffrey Vallance created quite a stir in 1978, when he bought a frozen chicken, took it to a pet cemetery in Los Angeles, and gave it a proper burial, complete with a silk-lined coffin and pallbearers. He named the chicken Blinky and chronicled the incident in the photo essay book, *Blinky: The Friendly Hen* (1979) and in a video. It is told that after the service, Vallance went to a nearby Howard Johnson's and ordered a "Chicken Special." Ten years later he exhumed Blinky to determine cause of death.

Other Chicken Artists

Ito Jakuchu (1716–1800) was one of Japan's most important artists, and the chicken was closely associated with his work. Jakuchu became a Zen Buddhist in his thirties and took on a deep commitment to the Zen principles of seeking spiritual enlightenment and ignoring temporal activities. In Jakuchu's paintings of chickens, the rooster or hen is the focal point. His chickens seem to possess human characteristics. Alone, they appear a metaphor for the individual, possibly Jakuchu himself, isolated and in search of spiritual enlightenment. In pairs or groups, Jakuchu's chickens seem to make eye contact with each other and exude a feeling of harmony. Jakuchu creates spectacular, colorful plumage, painting each feather with meticulous care. He also captures extremely subtle movement, frequently capturing a split-second twist or a turn of a chicken's head.

Columbian artist Fernando Botero (1932–) sculpted chickens and roosters in his typically delightful rotund style, with plump bodies and large legs. He also painted a picture of dead fowl in *The Kitchen Table* in 1970. When I first saw it, I must admit that it was not how I envisioned a Botero chicken would look. Given Botero's distinctive and humorous style of painting people, I had hoped for a comical plumper, with typical large body, small feet, and a peculiar little facial expression. However, the disappointment ended quickly when I realized the humor in this dead-fowl painting. Unlike most still lifes, which show rich, luscious fruits and vegetables set in a beautiful environment, Botero's reeks of vinegar and onions, showing a bloodied knife and a dead chicken with hanging entrails.

Cockfighting is reflected in the art of Emilio Rosado Mendez (1911–), a noted artist from Utuado, Puerto Rico. "The rooster is my favorite animal and throughout my life it has had a great influence on me," he once said. "As a child, I carved the image of roosters out of avocado pits, bananas and cardboard."

English fighting cocks are Mendez's personal passion and some of his most-famous artistic subjects. He is a dedicated *gallero*, a trainer and breeder of cockfighters, and his work portrays various positions of fighting roosters. Some crouch low in a fighting position, others are upright and proud. Rosado's vibrant colors reflect the rooster's vitality and strength and serve to honor this noble and fierce creature.

"When I warned [the French] that Britain would fight on alone whatever they did, their generals told their prime minister and his divided cabinet, 'In three weeks, England will have her neck wrung like a chicken.' Some chicken! Some neck!"
—Winston Churchill (1874–1965), in a speech to the Canadian Parliament, December 30, 1941

Chapter 4

Famous Clucks

Celluloid Chickens

Chickens have played significant roles in many of Hollywood's most celebrated movie moments. Their functions in these flicks are diverse. They are alluded to in notable quotations. Their symbolic value is often vital to a film's message. They can even be major characters in a film or serve as a catalyst for thought or action.

In *Angel Heart*, a dark and complex film rife with black magic, the character played by Mickey Rourke hates chickens and makes numerous derogatory remarks about them. Three times he says, "I've got a thing about chickens," and he asserts that "any dead chicken is a good chicken to me." As it turns out, Rourke's character happens to be an agent of the devil, so his aversion to the bird that is often associated with the Christian church is understandable.

Who can forget Jack Nicholson in *Five Easy Pieces*, attempting to order a piece of toast from a stern, uptight waitress, finally telling her to hold the chicken—between her thighs? Animal linguist Dr. Doolittle offers such sage advice as "Listen to the chickens." In *The Wizard of Oz*, the chickens on Dorothy's farm become the fussy little Munchkins in her dream. In James Dean's searing *Rebel Without a Cause*, the "chicken run" is the site of the film's pivotal fatal car crash. And in *South Pacific*, perky heroine Mitzi Gaynor sings that she was a "cock-eyed optimist."

Facing page:
Foghorn Leghorn
The venerable Foghorn Leghorn has appeared in such Warner Bros. cartoons as Crowing Pains, A Fractured Leghorn, Of Rice And Hen, The High And The Flighty, *and* Pullet Surprise. *He was also one of the Looney Tunes to hit the court with Michael Jordan in the movie* Space Jam. *(LOONEY TUNES characters, names and all related indicia are trademarks of Warner Bros. © 2002)*

Inset:
Chicken
Chicken is the star of the Cartoon Network's Cow and Chicken, *created by David Feiss. Chicken lives in the suburbs with his parents and his chubby, bovine younger sister Cow. Chicken tries to be tough and uses a large vocabulary, but suffers from an eleven year old's angst and a loathing of the opposite sex. (COW AND CHICKEN and all related characters and elements are trademarks of Cartoon Network © 2001. An AOL Time Warner Company. All Rights Reserved.)*

"The King's Eggs"

Carole Lombard and hubbie Clark Gable were Hollywood's most adorable chicken couple. Not only did they own chickens, but they also attempted an egg-laying operation with 600 Rhode Island Reds, whose eggs were sold under the label "The King's Eggs"—obviously capitalizing on the photogenic Clark's nickname. Even though Lombard allegedly sang the hens to sleep each night, the flock's production was sporadic. When the stars realized that their production cost per egg was one dollar, they abandoned the foul fowl venture.

Chickens, however, continued to inspire Lombard. The first day Gable was rehearsing the role of Rhett Butler in Gone with the Wind, *she sent him a knitted "cockwarmer" with a personal note "Don't let it get cold. Bring it home hot for me." In one of her early films, the reputation of Lombard's character is in question. Her image is not enhanced when she makes a grand entrance to a stuffy ladies' meeting saying, "Cock-a-doodle-doo, cock-a-doodle-doo, any cock'll doo." (Courtesy of Culver Pictures)*

In the animated film Chicken Run *(2000), Ginger (center) and her fellow hens eagerly anticipate their freedom from the Tweedy poultry farm. ("Chicken Run" courtesy of DreamWorks L.L.C., Pathe Image and Aardman Chicken Run Limited, reprinted with permission by DreamWorks Animation)*

The Blue Angel, by director Josef von Sternberg, is a chicken classic. This 1930 film chronicles the hellish marriage of Professor Rath (Emil Janning) and Lola (Marlene Dietrich), a sultry and seductive chanteuse at the Blue Angel Cafe. Professor Rath's life plummets after he loses his job as a well-respected educator and he becomes financially dependent on his unfaithful wife. An early scene shows their friend Kiepert, a slight of hand artist, make an egg appear from under Rath's nose. Lola begins to cluck like a hen, and Rath grins and suddenly crows like a cock. Later, penniless, Rath is forced to act on stage as Kiepert's assistant. Kiepert repeats the egg trick and humiliates Rath by breaking the egg on his head, demanding that he crow. He refuses. Meanwhile, Lola is offstage, madly embracing another fellow. Rath can stand no more. In a rage, he begins to crow, chases her into the dressing room, and lunges at her. As he strangles her, her death screams are mixed with his cock crowing.

Chickens are the obvious catalysts in the popular chicken farming movies. In each, the protagonists give up urban life in search of rural bliss by raising chickens. The first of these was entitled, surprisingly enough, *The Chickens* (1921). *The Egg and I*, Betty MacDonald's best-selling book, was made into a movie in 1947 starring Fred MacMurray and Claudette Colbert, whose characters move to an isolated chicken farm. Somehow, they survive every imaginable disaster that could befall such an inexperienced pair. In one memorable line, Bob (MacMurray) says, "Chickens sense things in people, you know." A less humorous movie, *The Fox* (1968), set in desolate Canada, adds a lesbian element to the isolated chicken farm theme.

No sibling rivalry
Brother Chicken and sister Cow enjoy a happy moment. (COW AND CHICKEN and all related characters and elements are trademarks of Cartoon Network © 2001. An AOL Time Warner Company. All Rights Reserved.)

"What's the use? Yesterday an egg, tomorrow a feather duster."
—Cartoonist Mark Fenderson (1873–1944), *The Dejected Rooster*

In Ingmar Bergman's *Shame* (1968), the chicken serves as a vehicle for a discussion between characters played by Max von Sydow and Liv Ullman. In jeopardy, they come to the important realization that they would be incapable of killing a chicken even to save themselves.

Part of the Italian film *Bread and Chocolate* (1973) by Franco Brusati takes place in a chicken slaughterhouse and in a converted chicken coop, where the family lives, eats, and even sleeps with the chickens.

The chickens in *Goin' South* (1978) symbolically mimic the sexual tension between outlaw Jack Nicholson and spinster Mary Steenburgen.

A silent movie by Charlie Chaplin, *The Gold Rush* (1925), and *Ma and Pa Kettle at Home* (1954) both showcase chickens throughout their story lines.

Tipped off that there was a chicken in *Nosferatu,* I rented the 1922 silent classic to see for myself. I barely endured the movie's ninety-three minutes with its interminable background music, before finally seeing a flashing one-second scene of a rooster crowing. At that point, I didn't care what it symbolized. However, when I rented the 1979 remake by Werner Herzog, I found an abundance of chickens portrayed in the film.

The Ghost and Mrs. Chicken (1966), which stars the bug-eyed actor Don Knotts, is a chicken film in name only. Knotts portrays a bumbling police officer, reminiscent of his television role in *The Andy Griffith Show,* who is afraid of just about everything. As such, he is the only "chicken" in the film.

Chicken Run (2000) is the first classic chicken film in the twenty-first century. Created by a crew of clever animators in England, the critically acclaimed film features a troop of endearing, handmade claymation chickens. Set on a poultry farm, which has all the grim aspects of a prisoner-of-war camp, the flock dreams of freedom. The hens, faced with the hard choice of either producing more eggs or being sent to the chopping block, plot their escape, led by the scrappy hen Ginger. The hens find themselves in deep trouble when the evil Mrs. Tweedy and her henpecked husband, owners of the farm, purchase a massive chicken-pie-making machine. An uncertain hope arrives in the form of a fast-talking Rocky, an American rooster on the lam from a carnival, who agrees to teach the girls how to fly to freedom—with mixed results.

Cartoon Chickens

Cow and Chicken is a creation of cartoon genius David Feiss and originally appeared on the Cartoon Network. The pilot was created in 1994, and since then fifty-two brilliant shows have been created. Feiss did raise chickens as a child, although he claims they were not the inspiration for the show. Instead, the idea came to him in the form of a bedtime story he told to his children, whose personalities loosely inspired the characters of Cow and her older brother Chicken.

The lyrics to the show's theme song acknowledge—but don't really explain—the strangeness of the sibling pair: "Mama had a Chicken, Mama had a Cow, Dad was proud, He didn't care how. Cow. Chicken. Cow and Chicken!" Other than the fact that they are farm animals, Cow and Chicken are typical suburban kids, with typical human parents and friends. They face all the typical challenges of youngsters, such as mean classmates, insensitive teachers, and a red devil. In one clever episode I watched, Chicken had the first-day-of-school jitters. Adding to his trepidation were bullies in gym class and a tyrannical gym teacher who made naked showers mandatory; his humiliation is complete when his feather suit is stolen. Clearly, *Cow and Chicken* addresses issues everyone, young and old, can relate to.

Super Chicken was a cartoon show produced by Jay Ward and Bill Scott, the creators of *Rocky and Bullwinkle*. Alas, only seventeen six-minute episodes were ever made between 1967 and 1968. The star of the show is Henry Cabot Henhaus III, the richest chicken in the world and an amateur scientist. His inept butler, Fred, a lion, is his sidekick. In each episode Henry would drink his Super Sauce and turn into the superhero known as Super Chicken. Fred would inevitably bumble the situation.

The famed film rooster Foghorn Leghorn appeared in the Warner Bros. cartoon, *Walky Talky Hawky.* Foghorn is a barnyard rooster with a thick Southern accent who is constantly beleaguered by his three nemeses: Henery Hawk, a chickenhawk who continually attempts to capture him for supper; Miss Prissy, who tries to lure him into matrimonial bliss; and the yellow chick, Eggbert who perpetually outsmarts him. He takes out his frustrations on the hapless Barnyard Dog, who is often the butt of his practical jokes. Directed by Robert McKimson, *Walky Talky Hawky* received an Oscar nomination.

Radio Chicken

The classic radio serial, *Chickenman*, was launched in 1966 under the creative wing of Chicago radio genius Dick Orkin. Employed as a shoe salesman for a large department store, the main character spends his weekends—his only two days off—striking terror into the hearts of criminals everywhere as the white-winged warrior called Chickenman. This hilarious series was an in-house production of WCFL-Radio in Chicago and began at the urging of Ken Draper, the station's program director. In the show, Orkin played the role of "Chickenman—the most fantastic crime fighter the world has ever known," as well as the police commissioner. Jim Runyon, host of a morning show, was the series' announcer, and Jane Roberts, a WCFL traffic reporter, portrayed Mrs. Helfinger and the Masked Mother. The series eventually played on more that 1,500 radio stations in the United States and overseas.

Chickenman

An artist's rendering of the radio hero Chickenman, "the most fantastic crime fighter the world has ever known." (© 2002 by DOCSI Corp. Used with permission from Dick Orkin)

Chickens in Classical Music

The Golden Cockerel is a Russian opera by Nikolai Rimsky-Korsakov (1844–1908), first performed in 1909. This satirical and once-banned piece is based on a fable by Aleksandr Pushkin, written in 1834.

The Golden Cockerel tells the dark tale of a great czar named Dadon, in his youth a ruthless ruler and later an aging king who wants nothing more than to live in peace. Unfortunately, peace is not at hand as his kingdom is constantly surprised and attacked by the enemy. He asks a sorcerer for help, which arrives in the form of a golden cockerel with the wisdom to warn the czar of danger. In return, the czar agrees to grant the sorcerer one wish. One day, without explanation, the cock cries "wolf," which sends the czar's sons on a wild goose chase. They disappear, and their bodies are later found by the czar. It appears that the princess of Shamakhan had something to do with their demise, and she then lures the czar into her romantic web. He takes her back to the kingdom only to find out that the sorcerer also has designs on her and demands her as his one wish. The czar, outraged by his request, knocks the sorcerer on the head and kills him, after which the princess promptly deserts the czar. The cock then flies down from its perch and kills the czar by pecking at his head.

Chickens have influenced other classical composers and pieces, including:

- Joseph Haydn (1732–1809). *The Hen Symphony #83* was named for its clucking second movement.
- Jean Philippe Rameau (1683–1764), *La Poule*
- Ottorino Respighi (1879–1936), *Birds*, with variations on *La Poule*
- Modest Petrovich Musorgsky (1839–1881). *Ballet of the Unhatched Chicks* humorously describes chicks hatching from their shells.
- Carl Nielsen (1865–1931), *Dance of the Cockerels*
- Charles Camille Saint-Saens (1835–1921). The first movement of his *Carnival of the Animals* is "Hens and Cocks."

The CD *Pass the Chicken and Listen*, with music by the Everly Brothers and produced by Chet Atkins, has a beautiful cover depicting chickens, but there aren't any tunes about the birds on the album.

Chickens in Music and Song

When you think of chicken music, one of first songs that comes to mind is the always-popular-at-weddings-and-at-German-festivals *Chicken Dance*. Surprisingly, this song is relatively contemporary. I had imagined that it would have played at the first Oktoberfest in Munich in 1810, which celebrated the marriage of Prince Ludwig I and Princess Therese von Sachsen-Hildburghausen. Instead, this dance song was written by Werner Thomas, a composer from Davos, Switzerland, in the early 1970s. The tune was originally called the *Duck Dance* and only later evolved into the *Chicken Dance* or, occasionally, *Dance Little Bird*. Gradually, it became a popular German heritage song in the United States.

In 1861, Stephen Foster, one of America's best-loved songwriters, was inspired to write a song about the Shanghai in the breed's honor called *Don't Bet Your Money on de Shanghai*.

> De Shanghai chicken when you put him in de pit
> He'll eat a loaf of bread up but he can't fight a bit
> De Shanghai fiddle is a funny little thing
> And ebry time you tune him up he goes ching! ching!
> Oh! de Shanghai!
> Don't bet your money on de Shanghai!
> Take de little chicken in de middle of de ring
> But don't bet your money on de Shanghai.

The Chicken Walk, by Irving Berlin, was another hit song. It was written in 1916, just before the dark days of World War I rolled over Tin Pan Alley.

> There's a dance that soon will be the talk
> Won't you kindly name it?
> It is called the Broadway Chicken Walk,
> Who's the one to claim it?
> Young and pretty girlies with Mary Pickford curlies,
> First started doing it in New York—that Chicken Walk.
> It's full of fun.
> Won't you tell us how it's done?
> Scratch the ground with your feet and then you gaze around
> Should you meet a millionaire, Don't stare.
> Just tell him you won't stop. Don't stop.
> Flap your wings. Start to talk about engagement ring
> And then you fly back to your coop.

The Rooster (Thoughts in a Hen Coop) was composed in 1925, with verses by John Kendrick Bangs and music by John Barnes Wells.

> I love to watch a rooster crow
> He's like so many men I know
> Who brag and bluster, ramp and shout
> And beat their manly chests without
> The first darn thing to crow about!

Chicken music

Although better known for the songs "Oh Susanna" and "Camp Town Races," Stephen Foster did not neglect the chicken craze in the mid 1800s. His humorous song about the Shanghai chicken does not flatter the breed.

Chicken-scratch music was created in Arizona's central and southern deserts more than a hundred years ago by the Pima and Tohono O'odham (formerly Papago) tribes. It got its name from an old style of O'odham dance, where the dancers kicked up their heels and, from a distance, sounded and looked like chickens scratching.

> "Hongry rooster don't cackle w'en he find a wum."
> "Rooster makes mo' racket dan de hin w'at lay de aig."
> —Joel Chandler Harris (1848–1908), *Uncle Remus: His Songs and His Sayings*

The Chicken or the Egg came from *The Stupendous Broadway Musical* in 1929.

Which come first? The chicken or the egg
The egg or the chicken or the chicken or the egg?
All my life I'd been in doubt
Which was the first to come out
Please won't someone answer me? on my knees I beg,
Which come first, the chicken or the egg, the egg or the
chicken or the chicken or the egg?

Harry B. Smith wrote the lyrics and Victor Herbert wrote the music for *The Hen and the Weather Vane* (1928). The song tells the sad tale of a bantam hen who was in love with a rooster-shaped weathervane.

A little bantam hen in a barnyard dwelt,
And a white little hen was she,
All the roosters thought her more than fair
As they wooed her on bended knee
But the bantam hen didn't care for men,
So their chances were but small:
She had love untold for the rooster bold
On top of a steeple tall
So looking up the whole day long,
That love sick banty sang this song
Weather vane! Weather vane! You're so far above me,
I can't expect 'twould be correct
For one so high to love me,
Weather vane! Weather vane!
Proud you are I see
But whether vain or not you are the one for me.

A Chicken Ain't Nothing but a Bird is a fox trot, written by Babe Wallace in 1940.

Ev'ry one's talking 'bout chicken—
Chicken's a popular word.
But any where you go you're bound to find—
A chicken ain't nothin' but a Bird
Some people call it fowl—That's the story I've heard
But let 'em call it this and let 'em call it that
A chicken ain't nothin'
But a Bird.

Other chicken-inspired music includes *Set My Chickens Free,* sung by country-music great Merle Haggard. In the world of blues, Patti LuPone sang *Ain't Nobody Here but Us Chickens*, written by Alex Kramer and Joan Whitney, and also recorded by Louis Jordan, Asleep at the Wheel, B. B. King, Lisa Stansfield, and many others. *If You Steal My Chickens You Can't Make 'em Lay* by Rediscovered Blues with Lightnin' Hopkins, Brownie McGhee, Terry Sonny, and Big Joe Williams was another blues hit. Rock n' roller Chuck Berry rocked with *Chicken Stuff,* and even the world of jazz crooned about poultry with songs like Harry Belafonte's *Chickens.* Cockfighting is celebrated in Western folk singer Tom Russell's contemporary tune, *Gallo del Cielo,* which tells of a young Mexican man attempting to win enough money with his fabled fighting rooster, "born in heaven as the legends say," to buy back the family ranch stolen by Pancho Villa.

Performing Chickens

Mike, the Headless Wonder Chicken, was immortalized in a *Life* magazine article in 1945. His existence as a plump, unsuspecting Wyandotte was about to end by means of an ax wielded by his owner, Lloyd Olsen of Fruita, Colorado. Though the ax did its job, the beheaded bird escaped. Lloyd found him the next day—still alive. Impressed with his chicken's determination to survive, Olsen decided to help him. The farmer took the bird to the University of Utah, where scientists determined that the ax missed Mike's jugular vein and a clot prevented him from bleeding to death. With an eyedropper, Olsen fed the plucky poultry grains and water through its neck, and Mike eventually grew to weigh eight pounds.

Billed as "The Headless Wonder Chicken," Mike set out on a national tour with the appropriate entourage led by Olsen. One night, at an unidentified motel in Arizona, Mike choked, and his distraught owner was unable to find the eyedropper to clear his feathered friend's esophagus. Mike expired, yet Olsen still came out okay, collecting the $10,000 insurance he carried on the bird. Mike's short life is still celebrated annually with a festival held the third weekend in May in Fruita.

On a family vacation trip to South Dakota a few years ago, I saw a baseball-playing chicken in action at the Black Hills Reptile Gardens in Rapid City, South Dakota. I have also had the humiliating experience of being outsmarted by a chicken playing tic-tac-toe at the same establishment. Realizing my lack of expertise at the game of poker, I chose not to be demoralized by Sticky Fingers Joe, a chicken known to beat real people at the game every time. (I still don't know how he does it.)

Literary Chickens

Chicken-inspired literature can be found in many cultures, and there are many great chicken tales that amuse and educate.

Aesop, perhaps the most famous of all fable writers, was a Greek slave who lived about 600 B.C. Best known for the tale of the devil-may-care hare and the plodding tortoise, Aesop also extracted great wisdom from the characters of hens and roosters.

For example, the *Cock and the Jewel* is the story of how a cock, while scratching up the straw in a farmyard in search of food for the hens, hit upon a jewel that by some chance had found its way there. "Ho!" he said, "You are a very fine thing, no doubt to those who prize you; but give me a barley-corn before all the pearls in the world." The moral of the story is that what is valuable to one person might be worthless to another.

A Woman and a Fat Hen tells about a woman who had a hen that laid an egg every day. She figured that if she gave the hen more food, it might be able to lay two eggs each day. Although the hen grew fat, it stopped laying eggs all together. The moral of that story is that someone who already has plenty but still wants more will never have enough. We should learn to be content with what we already have, lest we lose even that.

"Don't count your chickens before they are hatched" is the moral to Aesop's fable *The Milkmaid and Her Pail.*

"The early village cock hath twice done salutation to the morn."
—William Shakespeare, *Richard III*

Mother Carey's Chickens: Her Voyage to the Unknown Isle was an 1888 novel by G. Manville Fenn. However, Mother Carey's chickens weren't really chickens. Instead they were petrels, or birds that live on the ocean far from land and return to shore only during breeding season.

In *Pseudolus,* by Plautus, (c. 254–184 B.C.), a Roman comic poet, a character holds up an unintelligible love letter and declares, "By Hercules, do hens also have hands? For a chicken wrote this."

Other Aesop chicken fables include:

Two Young Men and a Cock
The Cat and the Cock
The Fighting Cock and the Eagle
The Hen and the Cat
The Dog, the Cock and the Fox
The Fox and the Cock
The Cat, the Cock and the Young Mouse
The Falcon and the Hen
The Fighting Cocks and the Turkey
A Cock Boasting of His Services
The Ass, the Cock, and the Lion

Geoffrey Chaucer (1340?–1400) immortalized the character of Chanticleer in "The Nun's Priest's Tale," one of his famous *Canterbury Tales*. In the story, Chanticleer, the cock, is characterized by typical rooster traits: He is elegant and intellectual, egotistical and vain, but likable enough. He is a polygamist, with seven hen wives, although he favors Pertelote, the fairest among them. In the tale, Chanticleer tells Pertelote he was "soore afright" by a premonition of a beast "lyk a hound," and she reprimands him for his cowardliness. In fact, she cites the meaninglessness of dream, and Chanticleer responds with a slew of classical and intellectual references. Sir Russel Fox then lures Chanticleer away from the barnyard with flattery and carries him off. He is ultimately outwitted by Chanticleer, who eventually escapes. "The Nun's Priest's Tale" is often considered to be the most intellectual of Chaucer's tales with Chanticleer being the wisest of his characters.

William Shakespeare often refers to chickens throughout his plays. For example, in *Macbeth,* on hearing of the savage slaughter of his wife and children, MacDuff cries out, "Oh hell-kite! All? What! all my pretty chickens and their dam, at one fell swoop?"

The Taming of the Shrew includes the following exchange between the two main characters.

> Katharina: What is your crest? A coxcomb?
> Petruchio: A combless cock, so Kate will be my hen.
> Katharina: No cock of mine. You crow too like a craven [a cock that will not fight]. The cock, that is the trumpet to the morn. Doth with his lofty and shrill sounding throat awake the god of day.

In *Hamlet*, when Marcellus tells of the disappearance of old Hamlet's ghost, he repeats the belief that the cock sings throughout Christmas Eve to paralyze the witches.

> It faded on the crowing of the cock.
> Some say that ever 'gainst that season comes
> Wherein our Savior's birth is celebrated,
> The bird of dawning singeth all night long;
> And then, they say, no spirit dare stir abroad.
> The nights are wholesome; then no planets strike,
> No fairy takes, nor witch hath power to charm,
> So hallowed and so gracious is the time.

The seer most often quoted in the supermarket tabloids, Nostradamus (1503–1566) knew that the cock would be of national importance to France, as he prophesied in the *Oracles of Nostradamus.*

> The grand celibate shall die three
> leagues from the Rhone;
> The dejected brothers shall fly
> tumult:
> For war shall make a most horrible
> throne
> For the three brothers of France by
> the Cock and Eagle.

Allegedly, his prognostication refers to the pope dying, Louis XVIII and Charles X being overthrown, and the French Revolution inflicting havoc on the three brothers—Louis XVI, Louis XVIII, and Charles X. (The cock and the eagle refer to the *Coq Galois* and the Napoleonic eagle.)

In 1606, this rhyme was the first utterance of a young girl whose tongue had been cut out, as told in the story of *The Most Cuvell and Bloody Murther committed by an Innkeeper's Wife called Annis Dell and her Sonne George Dell.*

> Cock a Doodle Doo
> Cock a Doodle Doo!
> My dame has lost her shoe.
> My master's lost his fiddlestick,
> And knows not what to do.

According to the story, Anthony James, a three-year-old boy, was murdered at Bishop's Hatfield, in Herefordshire. The murder was witnessed by his four-year-old sister. To prevent her from naming them, the killers ripped out her tongue. Three years later, the girl, after hearing the cock crow, miraculously recovered her speech. Her first words were "Cock a doodle doo,

The Town Musicians of Bremen

The Brementown Musicians are often portrayed in art. This beautiful porcelain figure is a piece of Hutschenreuther china from Bavaria. (Figure owned by Art and Heide Wetzel; photograph by Michael Cleary)

In the tragic tome *Tess of the d'Urbervilles,* by Thomas Hardy (1840–1928), the cock crows three times on the wedding day of Tess and Angel—an omen of their ill-fated marriage.

"I don't know which is more discouraging, literature or chickens." —E. B. White (1899–1985), in a letter to James Thurber

Peggy hath lost her shoe." Later, the phrase evolved to "my dame has lost her shoe." After regaining her voice, she was taken to the local judge, to whom she recounted the story of her brother's murder by Annis Dell and her son.

Hans Christian Anderson (1805–1875), Denmark's most famous storyteller, wrote fairy tales for young and old. With his satirical tale *It's Perfectly True,* Anderson perpetuates the stereotype of hens as gossipy and malicious and also reveals the dynamic of rumors. The allegory also delves into the vanity of women who go to great lengths to attract men by altering their appearance.

In the story, a respectable hen jokes that "the more I pick myself, the more beautiful I will become," when one of her feathers happens to fall out. This innocent comment is overheard by a malicious hen that starts a rumor rolling. She claims that there is a hen that is going to pluck out her feathers to look more attractive to the roosters. The next version of the rumor tells of the hen picking out all her feathers while the rooster watches her. Then the number of hens involved is exaggerated—some say there are two hens who have plucked out their feathers. Eventually the story grows until it says that three hens have died of unrequited love. Finally the tale arrives back to the original hen house saying that five hens have plucked out all their feathers to prove who was the thinnest, after which they all pecked each other to death. According to the tale, this story was then published in the newspaper as fact.

The Grimm brothers, Jakob (1785–1863) and Wilhelm (1786–1859), were scholars interested in preserving the culture and history of Germany in the early nineteenth century. By collecting and compiling German folk tales, they captured the Teutonic spirit, preserved its rich oral history, and instilled national pride in German heritage.

The best-known chicken in the Grimms' tales is the cock of *The Town Musicians of Bremen,* who overheard that he was to become supper because he supposedly had outlived his usefulness. He subsequently joined a group of other over-the-hill animals—a donkey, a dog, and a cat—whose thankless masters had plotted their demise, as well. The friends headed to Bremen to become musicians but wound up encountering a group of robbers in a house. They scared off the bandits by climbing atop each other to look in a window and then making a raucous noise. The animals took over the bandits' house and lived happily ever after.

Artwork often depicts the Bremen pyramid of animals as they are said to be in the original story with the donkey on the bottom, the dog on top of him, the cat atop the dog, and the cock on the back of the cat. Later depictions show a variety of animals involved; however, the cock is consistently on the top of the heap.

From his teen years, American author Mark Twain (1835–1910) had a keen interest in poultry. In 1875, he was made an honorary member of the Western New York Poultry Society. In his book of essays, *Sketches New and Old*, "Raising Poultry" is actually a tongue-in-cheek letter of thanks for his honorary membership. He begins, "Seriously, from early youth, I have taken an especial interest in the subject of

And sounding in advance its victory,
My song jets forth so clear, so
proud, so peremptory,
That the horizon,
seized with a rosy trembling,
Obeys me.
—Edmond Rostand, *Chantecler*

Chantecler
An appropriately handsome, confident rooster graces the cover of this edition of Chantecler, *published in 1910.*

Hensure hens

These hensure hens are picketing for women's rights in the days before the Nineteenth Amendment. I question the "wise" old owl looking down upon them.

"He was like a cock who thought the sun had risen to hear him crow." —George Eliot (1819–1880), *Adam Bede*

poultry-raising, and so this membership touches a ready sympathy in my breast." In his usual quirky style, Twain discusses his poultry-rearing techniques, including the practice of "raising them off a roost by burning lucifer matches under their noses." He mentions the Shanghai rooster as "donkey-voiced" and needing a lasso to corral the birds. Twain described some Black Spanish chickens that cost between thirty-five and fifty dollars, with each of their eggs selling for a dollar to a dollar and a half. Yet they were "so unwholesome that the city physician seldom or never orders them for the work-house."

Better known for his play about a romantic with a huge proboscis, *Cyrano de Bergerac*, French poet and dramatist Edmond Rostand (1868–1918) also wrote a play about an egotistical rooster called *Chantecler* in 1910. Chantecler is an idealist, who believes that he has a mystical power because his song makes the sun rise. He is also all too human and falls passionately in love with Pheasant Hen, the archetype of a woman with a mission—a desire to possess Chantecler. She tells him, "You can be all in all to me, but nothing to the dawn." Chantecler succumbs to her seduction and becomes her henpecked husband, not waking the sun because of her petty jealousy. Though the play dealt with many other issues—friendship, idealism, persecution, loyalty, honor—it was not a critical success, and Rostand started his retirement soon after.

P. G. Wodehouse (1881–1975) first wrote his hilarious short novel *Love Among the Chickens* in 1906, setting it on a Dorsetshire chicken farm in Devon, England. In the story, the outrageous schemer and blowhard, Stanley Featherstonehaugh

Ukridge, convinces his friend Garnet that fame and fortune can be achieved by raising chickens. His plan is simple.

> I've thought it over, Laddie, and it's as clear as mud. No expenses, large profits, quick return. Chickens, eggs and the money streaming in faster than you can bank it. Winter and summer, underclothing, my bonny boy, lined with crackling Bradbury's. It's the idea of a lifetime. Now listen to me for a moment. You get your first hen on tick [loan]. Anybody will be glad to let you have a hen on tick. Well, then, you let this hen, this first original hen, this on-tick-hen—you let it set and hatch chickens.
>
> Suppose you have a dozen hens. Very well, then. When each of the dozens has a dozen chickens, you send the old hens back to the chappies you borrowed them from, with thanks for kind loan: and there you are, starting business with a hundred and forty-four free chickens to your name.

As might be expected, *Love Among the Chickens* went amuck.

Cocksure Women and Hensure Men (1928) was written by D. H. Lawrence (1885–1930). In this politically incorrect piece, Lawrence described, generalized, and categorized women into two types: the demure and the dauntless. He claimed the old-fashioned, demure wife, maiden, or lover as still "the ideal" and "hensure" and deplored the confidence of the dauntless or modern woman, vilifying her as "cocksure." He found cocksure women tragic because in-

Chicken cartoon

This cartoon by Leigh Rubin is one of my favorites. (Reprinted by permission of Leigh Rubin and Creators Syndicate, Inc.)

While the cock with lively din
Scatters the rear of darkness thin,
And to the stack, or the barn door,
Stoutly struts his dames before.
Oft list'ning how the hounds
and horn
Surely rouse the slumb'ring morn.
—John Milton (1608–1674),
L'Allegro

stead of "laying an egg" (having children), they "lay a vote and other unhatchable things." He said the contemporary female was so busy "out-manning" the man that at the end of her life she will finally realize that she is a hen and not a cock and that she has missed her life calling—motherhood—altogether, ending up with nothing.

Before he became known as a great American poet, Robert Frost (1874–1963) raised Wyandottes on a Massachusetts farm and wrote short stories for two New England poultry magazines, *Farm-Poultry* and *The Eastern Poultryman*. "A Start in the Fancy" tells the story of a farmer who is the first in his community to purchase a ten-dollar pullet for show instead of just for eggs. His neighbors mercilessly tease him about his flight of fancy, and their attitude, combined with the hen's failure to produce prizewinning offspring, nearly drive him to despair. He is about to give up the enterprise when one day a visitor asks him how much he wants for some of his birds. In a last effort to salvage his enterprise—and his pride—he hesitantly names the outrageous price of five dollars a bird.

> There was silence for awhile. Then the visitor turned a quizzical look on the trembling man.
>
> "How many birds have you ever sold for five dollars?" he said.
>
> "Ask me how many I ever bought for five dollars," said the man.
>
> Again there was a silence. Then the visitor said, brushing his knees, "I guess you're new to the business. Just to encourage you I'm going to give you five apiece for the five. You round them up and crate them now, and let me see you off to the station before I go."
>
> The man nearly dropped down dead. He experienced a sudden return to the courage of his convictions. Before he had quite recovered from the shock, he found himself back from the station, poorer by the loss of five good cockerels, (which he now for the first time really appreciated) but richer by twenty-five dollars, and some new ideas. He was saved to the fancy.

The pioneering poultryman is further vindicated when, two years later, "Excitement over the new poultryculture struck the town with a rush," and all the neighbors who made fun of his fancy fowl suddenly become poultry fanciers themselves.

In 1937, farmer and writer E. B. White (1899–1985) wrote a funny essay entitled "Soothing the Chickens." In it, he describes how a Massachusetts poultry farmer found a novel way to enhance his chickens' egg output.

> He discovered that if his hens were disturbed by a sudden noise in the night, egg production fell off sharply next day. So now he keeps a radio going quietly night and day among his hens, immunizing them against the virus of sound. It works perfectly. Let a door squeak on its hinges; the hens accept it as a sound effect. Somehow it gives us a secret, deep pleasure to know that a dramatized news broadcast, aimed to unnerve the rest of us, is definitely reassuring to a lot of sleepy fowl, dreaming of hawks and weasels in a hen house far away.

In the classic novel by Betty Smith, *A*

Tree Grows in Brooklyn (1943), a father in 1912 Brooklyn takes the family savings account and buys chickens. He shelters the birds in the backyard, hoping to make a fortune.

> The first night, twenty starving cats came over the fence and killed and ate many chickens. The second night, the Italians climbed the fence and stole more. The third day, the policeman came and said it was against the law to keep chickens in a yard in Brooklyn.

The discouraged dad sells the rest of his flock and buys canaries.

Chicken Poems

Jean de la Fontaine (1621–1695) was a famous French poet noted for his verses inspired by Aesop's works. *The Hen that Laid the Golden Egg* is based on Aesop's fable *A Woman and a Fat Hen.*

> No better fable was ever written
> For those whom the money bug has bitten
> Than that of the man whose hen could lay
> A golden egg for him every day.
> He cut her open from stem to stern
> To get the goldmine, only to learn
> That his hen inside was like every hen
> And he, more the fool, was poor again.
> Many a duffer these days will euchre
> Himself right out of a pot of lucre
> By caring too much about the stuff.
> So always remember, enough's enough.

Cock-Throwing is a nasty traditional children's poem from the Victorian era, popular before cockfighting and animal baiting were outlawed in Britain.

> Cock a doodle doo! 'Tis
> the bravest game,
> Take a cock from his dame,
> And bind him to a stake:
> How he struts! how he throws!
> How he swaggers! how he crows!
> As if the day newly brake.
> How his mistress cackles
> Thus to find him in shackles
> And tied to a pack-thread garter!
> Oh, the bears and the bulls
> Are but corpulent gulls
> To the valiant Shrovetide martyr!

Chickens in Children's Literature

Chickens are immortalized in many children's books and stories, the most notable characters being the Little Red Hen, Henny-Penny, and Chicken Little.

The Little Red Hen exudes the Protestant work ethic, as she single-handedly runs the household, without a morsel of aid from her lazy cat, dog, and mouse friends. When she asks for a little help planting, sowing, and milling wheat to bake a cake, she is met with a chorus of "Not I." But in the end, she gets her cake and eats it too.

> All by myself
> I planted the wheat,
> I tended the wheat,
> I cut the wheat,
> I took the wheat to the mill
> To be ground into flour.
> All by myself

---

so much depends
upon
a red wheel
barrow
glazed with rain
water
beside the white
chickens
—William Carlos Williams (1883–1963), *The Red Wheelbarrow*

Thirty thousand kazoo players convened in Cincinnati, Ohio, at the Oktoberfest-Zinzinnati 2000, the nation's largest Oktoberfest, to set a world's record for the largest Chicken Dance and Kazoo Band. The Cincinnati City Council had to suspend a noise ordinance to allow this history-making feat to occur.

I gathered the sticks,
I built the fire,
I mixed the cake.
And
All by myself
I am going to eat it!

There are various versions of *Henny-Penny* and *Chicken Little*, but in each the title chicken panics when an object falls on her head. She assumes the worst, that "the sky is falling." So she sets off to tell the king of the predicament. Along the way, all of her friends join her: Cocky Locky, Ducky Daddles, Goosey Loosey, Turkey Lurkey, and Gander Pander. They all believe the end is near, perpetuating her story. In some versions, the tale ends when the animals meet their shrewd nemesis, Foxy Loxy, who gobbles them up. (Many versions do not have such an unhappy ending, and the characters survive their meeting with the fox.)

Beatrix Potter (1866–1943) escaped from the world of Victorian repression to an imaginary place: an enchanted world of animals. Potter, one of England's most noted illustrators of children's books, favors rabbits and squirrels in her stories. While the character development of her chickens is limited, chickens do appear in such tales as *The Tale of Mrs. Tiggy-Winkle, Ginger and Pickles*, and various others.

Chicken Sites and Attractions

The Chicken Ranch is a famous bordello near Las Vegas. Originally established in 1905 in La Grange, Texas, the bordello earned its name by accepting chickens in lieu of cash during the Depression. The Chicken Ranch was forced to close by a Houston reporter Marvin Zindler, who wrote exposés about it in 1973. Yet its legend lives on in the Broadway musical *The Best Little Whorehouse in Texas*, which was later made into a movie.

In 1976, the establishment was reborn as a new Chicken Ranch near "Sin City" Vegas, expanding its reputation to be "The Best Little Whorehouse in the West." Adjacent to the Chicken Ranch is the Leghorn Bar.

In the late 1800s, gold seekers traveled to Alaska in search of their fortunes. Many settled near the South Fork of the Forty Mile River where the willow ptarmigan, now the state bird, was abundant. In 1902, the town needed a name when it was about to become incorporated. "Ptarmigan" was suggested, but since no one could spell the word, they decided on "Chicken."

The National Poultry Museum at the Agriculture Center in Bonner Springs, Kansas, is preserving the history and importance of the American poultry industry. Loyl Stromberg from Pine River, Minnesota, is the force behind the National Poultry Museum. A man after my own heart, Loyl is an avid collector of chicken art and artifacts. His lifelong career in the chicken industry and his love of chickens has resulted in numerous books, culminating with his comprehensive *Poultry of the World* (1996).

In 1996, a friend and I made a pilgrimage from Milwaukee to Wayne, Nebraska, in search of an enlightening chicken experience. We were not disappointed. The Wayne Chicken Show has been an annual event since 1981 and is usually held on the second Saturday in July. It began as an arts and crafts show, and the chicken was chosen as its centerpiece due to its universality and the potential for frivolity.

Festival activities at the 1996 show included the chicken flying contest. For a dollar, each contestant chose a chicken, which was then placed in a mailbox high above the ground. The chickens were urged to fly with the gentle prodding of toilet plungers. My chicken lost. In fact, it emerged backward and fell uninjured to the ground. The winner soared like an eagle and landed in a pine tree on the other side of the park.

Other highlights included a street parade with the partially clothed "Chickendale Dancers" and the "Chicken Coupe," a 1967 Cadillac Coupe DeVille painted egg yoke yellow and sporting a twelve-foot glass rooster called Sasquawk on the trunk. There was also an egg drop contest in which the contestants attempted to catch eggs dropped from on high without breaking them; a beak contest in which human noses were awarded prizes based on proportion, cleanliness, texture, and "general beauty"; a chicken egg contest showcasing the biggest, smallest, and oddest eggs; a chicken song contest; a chicken calling contest where humans tried to lure chickens with odd noises and gestures; and a "cluck off" where prizes were awarded for the best impression of a chicken. (The rules for the latter specify that contestants can imitate a hen or a rooster, but not both. Points are awarded for authenticity, vocal projection, duration, and animation.) For chicken lovers and anyone who enjoys something different, the Wayne Chicken Show is a must.

Ultimate chicken costume

Why did the chicken cross the road? To see Jim Stafford, of course. Having watched comic/musician Stafford in frenetic action, I can attest that he thrills and delights his audiences at the Jim Stafford Theatre in the down-home music capital of the United States, Branson, Missouri. Not only does he sport the most fantastic glittering white chicken suit I have ever seen, he transports the audience with his hilarious comedy, his special effects, and his hit song Don't be Chicken When it's Time to Crow. *It's a show you won't want to miss. (Reproduced with permission from Jim and Ann Stafford)*

Chapter 5

Household Chickens

If you are not fortunate enough to live in an area that permits real chickens to roam your backyard, there is one solution: You can fill your house with chickenalia.

I define chickenalia as a "chicken object" or *objet de poulet*—an artifact that is formed in the shape of a chicken or bears the image of a chicken. An old wives' tale asserts that a chicken object in the home brings good luck. If that holds true, I should be the luckiest person in the world. Our home is replete with chickens—inside, outside, in the kitchen, in the living room, in the dining room, in the bathroom, on wallpaper, on towels, on lampshades, on tiles, in wall art. Our indoor flock is made out of porcelain, papier-mâché, wood, tin, brass, glass, and almost every other known material. Images of chickens adorn plates, lamps, pillows, glasses, furniture, wastebaskets, kitchen gadgets, doorstops, baskets, cache-pots, pitchers, vases, aprons. Chicken shapes inspire salt and pepper shakers, tureens, statues. The list goes on and on.

Facing page:
Wedgwood chickens
A hawk looming overhead, a defiant crowing cock, and the baby chicks scurrying under the protective wing of their mother hen are depicted on this chicken-inspired Wedgwood plate. (Photograph by Michael Cleary)

Inset:
Red rooster advertising
The A. Levy & J. Zentner Company of California used the image of a red rooster on its crate labels beginning in the 1930s. Others inspired by the red rooster: a winery in British Columbia; a swinger's club in Las Vegas; a guesthouse in Key West, Florida; a radio show called Blues from the Red Rooster Lounge*; an inn in Ellsworth, Maine; a Viagra alternative; an inn in Indiana's Amish country; a blues/rock band in Bristol, England; a café in Anthony, Texas; a pub and grill in Barbados, West Indies; an antique shop in Carver, Minnesota; a CD by Sam Cooke; a painting by Marc Chagall; a wine bar and café in Chicago; an organic fertilizer; and a song by Willie Dixon, sung by the Grateful Dead.*

Chickenalia from Around the World

Ceramic chickens made of porcelain, pottery, and stoneware are varied and beautiful, and throughout the world, they appear in every imaginable shape and size, with richly varied patterns and designs.

Porcelain originated in China in the first half of the ninth century. Forty beautiful decorative pieces were sent to the awe-struck sultan of Damascus in 1171, who immediately wondered how these beautiful objects were made. The secret was in the kaolin (a fine, white clay), feldspar (a crystalline mineral), quartz, and a sand found in the Far East.

It was not until the beginning of the eighteenth century that European potters were able to create a product that resembled the fine Chinese porcelain. A German businessman named Boettger discovered kaolin and feldspar near Meissen, Germany, and started the famous Meissen factory in 1710. It is said that the factory workers were imprisoned to guard the secret, but escapes were inevitable and soon other factories popped up. Now only china made in Meissen can be called Meissen and is identified by a famous logo of crossed swords. Meissen chickens are the crème de la crème of chickenalia. They are exquisite in their rich colors and fine detail. Other companies in Germany, such as Rosenthal and Goebel, also created beautiful ceramic chicken figurines.

Meissen

La crème de la crème of porcelain, this Meissen rooster is a beautiful example of the ultimate chicken porcelain. (Property of Art and Heide Wetzel, photograph by Michael Cleary)

Milk glass china

Milk glass covered chickens come in every imaginable color, shape, and size. These are a few from my collection. (Photograph by Michael Cleary)

France is filled with beautiful *objets de poulet,* including many made of faience, a tin-glazed earthenware pottery. Usually identified by the city or region where it was produced (Quimper, Blois, Gien, Desvres, Malicorne, Boulogne, Angouleme), faience has been produced in France since the seventeenth century. Roosters are a common motif in the Quimper product line.

Limoges was a prolific center of porcelain chickenalia in France. Many factories there began production in the mid-nineteenth century. Beautiful dinnerware with chicken motifs was made, as were well-known hinged boxes, many adorned with chickens in various shapes and sizes.

Milk glass was originally defined as opaque white glass, but manufacturers often made it in other colors so the term has expanded. First made in Venice in the fourteenth or fifteenth century, milk glass became popular throughout Europe and soon made its way to the United States. The ubiquitous milk glass hens in nests come in every imaginable shape, size, and color. Some have straight heads. Others are cocked. Some are sitting on a basket weave, with others on a smooth nest. They have painted heads or can be a solid color. Both the hens in nests and covered roosters became especially popular in England and France and reached the height of their popularity in the United States from 1870 to 1880. Milk glass hens on nests were often distributed as premiums around the turn of the century. They are still manufactured today, and in addition to being decorative, they are useful for holding candy or other small objects. Chickens also adorn milk-glass plates.

Beautiful chicken china also hails from England. Wedgwood, reputed to be among the world's most successful pottery companies, has several dinnerware lines inspired by the beauty of the chicken. The firm was founded by Josiah Wedgwood in 1759. Today, the Wedgwood Group is one of the largest fine china and earthenware manufacturers in the world.

Torquay is a small town in southern England near Devon where high-quality clay was discovered in 1869. Watcombe, the first factory there, opened the next year. Its success sparked many other companies, all producing high-quality porcelains. But in the 1920s, the industry there changed. Vacationers and day-trippers came to the beautiful palm-treed area and wanted inexpensive memorabilia to take home. To cater to the public's craving for souvenirs and love of cheesy sayings, the companies simplified their designs and added mottos, from the profound to the humorous. Called "mottoware," these popular ceramic bowls, cups, and other containers were made until 1962, and the chicken was a popular image on them.

Another very exquisite line of chicken figurines is made by Herend, a company founded in Herend, Hungary, by Moritz Fischer in 1839. The Herend roosters come in varying shapes, sizes, and styles.

There is a famous Italian pitcher design that dates back to the Italian Renaissance and is still being produced. In 1478, the leading family in Florence was the Medici family. Led by patriarch Lorenzo the Magnificent and his younger brother Guillano, the Medicis were beneficent landlords and often threw large parties for their workers. At one such event, at a town called Gallina (conveniently meaning "hen"), the Pazzis, the most serious rival of the Medicis, plotted the assassination of Guillano. Knowing he would overindulge at the festivities, they planned to murder him in his drunken slumber. But they overlooked the fact that the town was filled with chickens, who sounded the alarm and woke Guillano and his guards when the Pazzis invaded. Thankful to the chickens, Guillano ordered his artisans to create a ceramic pitcher design in the shape of a chicken, which he had made into wine vessels and given to the peasants of the town and to his friends. It is now a custom in Italy to give such a pitcher as a housewarming gift to protect homeowners from danger.

Salt and pepper chickens

This is a pair from my many chicken salt and pepper shakers. It is from Germany, made by the Goebel factory. (Photograph by Michael Cleary)

The Portuguese rooster, called the *Galo de Barcelo*, has been adopted by the Portuguese tourist bureau as its official emblem. This stylized rooster is recognizable by its oversized comb and tail, and it is ubiquitous in Portuguese pottery and handiwork. The choice of the rooster as a national icon is based in legend. In the town of Barcelos, in northwestern Portugal, a pilgrim on his way to Santiago do Compostela was accused of theft, arrested, and sentenced to be hanged. He prayed to the Virgin Mary and to St. James prior to an audience with the sentencing judge, who happened to be eating chicken. The prisoner declared that the rooster on the judge's plate would rise up and crow as proof of his innocence. The rooster did his miraculous duty, and the pilgrim was spared.

Throughout the history of the United States, the chicken has inspired many Ameri-

A typical Portuguese rooster

The oversized and stylized comb is a feature of the Portuguese rooster, a symbol adopted by the Portuguese tourist bureau as the country's emblem. (Photograph by Michael Cleary)

Paper egg cartons that hold a dozen eggs were created in 1886.

Chickens from around the world

This is just one of my many chicken nooks, filled with an international flock. The two largest pieces are a large white rooster statue (Italy) and a Wedgwood platter with Chantecler pattern (England). The smaller figurines, from left to right across the front, were made by Herend (Hungary), Limoges (France), Rosenthal (Germany), and Quimper (France). This corner also includes salt and pepper shakers (Germany) and a cock and fox netsuke *(Japan). (Photograph by Ricky Heldt)*

Torquay pottery

Torquay pottery was made in Devon, on the southern coast of England as early as 1867. "Mottoware" was introduced in the late nineteenth century to accommodate the influx of tourists wanting a souvenir of their trip. The back of this cup states "Hear all, See all, Say Nothing"—a difficult task for the oft-crowing rooster. (Photograph by Michael Cleary)

can companies to create plates, planters, figures, and other chickenalia. Companies such as Blue Ridge, Stangl, Metlox, Lefton, Hull, Royal Copley, Homer Laughlin, and others created chicken china and other chickenalia in the twentieth century, some of which is now very collectible.

Japanese *netsukes* are miniature figures carved of ivory, wood, and other materials. They were originally created for a utilitarian purpose. Since kimonos were pocketless, the figures were used to secure pouches containing personal belongings. *Netsukes* are identified by having two holes through which cords pass and attach to the *obi* (kimono sash). Since their origins in the fourteenth century, *netsukes* have evolved into a highly sophisticated art form with endless designs, including historical references, folklore, occupations, zodiac signs, animals, masks, and even explicit sexual symbols. *Netsukes* are often shaped like chickens, notably the cock of folklore.

Chickens around the fireplace

My living room and fireplace make a perfect display area for more *chickens. On the wall is a beautiful 1910 poster given to me by a friend. The mantel boasts ceramic chickens from Italy, China, France, and Portugal. (Photograph by Ricky Heldt)*

A Herend pair

Herend china is hand painted and made in Hungary. (Photograph by Michael Cleary)

A chicken couple

This Lefton chicken pair is from my collection. They were made between 1953 and 1971. (Photograph by Michael Cleary)

Sweet-smelling chicken
Avon cosmetics came in bottles with hundreds of shapes and sizes, including roosters. (Photograph by Michael Cleary)

"Colonel" Harland Sanders made his Kentucky Fried Chicken a household name when he started the company at age sixty-five with a $105 Social Security check. KFC is now owned by Pepsico and has annual sales of $8.9 billion.

Chickens in Advertising

Chicken images were often used to promote the United States chicken industry, but they were also used as symbols or simply appealing images to advertise other products. Artist Ben Austrian created one of the earliest American trademarks in 1886—the Bon Ami chick with its companion slogan "Hasn't Scratched Yet!" Bon Ami is a soap product, and the slogan referred to the fact that a newborn chick will not scratch for food immediately after hatching, since it is able to live for a few days on the nutrients of the yolk that sustained it within the egg. Later, to increase sales in the 1980s, the Bon Ami firm launched a national magazine advertising campaign with the slogan "Never Underestimate the Cleaning Power of a 94 Year-Old Chick With a French Name."

The Kellogg's Corn Flakes rooster greets the breakfast eater with a smile. Created in the late 1950s, Cornelius (a.k.a. Corny) is a green rooster with a red comb and yellow beak. Internationally known, in Columbia he is referred to as "Cornelio" and in Great Britain, "Choc-o-doodle-do."

Sakonnet Wine in Little Compton, Rhode Island, capitalizes on the Rhode Island rooster for its image. Haan Winery from South Australia also uses a beautiful image of a rooster on its label. The rooster is used as advertising at the Courage Brewery in England with the logo "Take Courage." The label of Red Rooster Ale is inspired by the rooster, as well as that of Cock Beer, Cock Master Malt (Extra Smooth), Cockle Extract Ale, CockSucka, and Cold Cock. Cockspur Fine Rum from the Barbados, West Indies, also sports a rooster on its label.

Most famous for the discovery of Elvis, the Sun Record Company with the well-known crowing rooster logo was founded in 1949 by Memphis disc jockey Sam Phillips. Johnny Cash, Roy Orbison, Carl Perkins, Charlie Rich, Carl Mann, Bill Justis, and Jerry Lee Lewis shared the Sun label during the 1950s.

Cigarette packs began to include cards in the late 1800s, because the flimsy paper package needed a piece of cardboard to help it hold its shape. This piece of cardboard became known as a "stiffener," and it was often decorated with advertising and designs to attract customers. At that time, most of the smokers were men, and the messages on the cards catered to them. For example, in Britain between 1899 and 1902, tobacco companies catered to the public interest in the Boer War by producing cards with regiments, uniforms, war leaders, incidents, and events from the war as it unfolded. Cigarette card popularity continued through both world wars. The topics expanded from war themes and beautiful women to include every conceivable subject: animals, birds, historical figures, sporting subjects, motor cars, hobbies, flowers—and chickens.

Charles Pathé created a cinema industry with none other than the proud Gallic rooster as its emblem. A visionary rather than an artist, Pathé created newsreels, a home-movie camera company called Pathé Baby, and another company called Pathé Rural that provided movies to small villages. All these enterprises carried the distinguished rooster as a herald of their success.

Don't take away my rooster

A very disgruntled, though cherubic, boy holds a rooster in this early-twentieth-century advertisement for the Great Atlantic & Pacific Tea Company. I haven't quite determined the message.

Pathé Film

The coq is ubiquitous as a symbol in France and serves as the logo for many companies, including the Pathé Film Company and its subsidiaries.

Beauty secrets

Wilson's claimed its egg shampoo was "the greatest known Scalp Cleanser, Nature's best assistant" and left hair "soft, fluffy, and beautiful, ready for nature which does all the hair growing." Perhaps the company knew the age-old beauty secret that suggested washing your hair in raw eggs to give it shine.

Clever clip

In this 2002 television commercial, Jim Perdue, chairman of Perdue Farms, introduces himself, then says, "People say I'm obsessed with chickens. You could say I'm passionate. But obsessed? That's ridiculous." As he continues to expound on the quality of Perdue chicken, the camera moves around a home—much like my own—filled with chicken art, chicken china, chicken lamps, and other chickenalia. The commercial inspired many new ideas, too: I could certainly use a closet full of chicken hangers, a chicken showerhead, and maybe even a chicken tattoo. (Used with permission from Perdue Farms)

Chicken cigarette cards

Now very collectible, these cigarette cards were once a premium in cigarette packages. The cards showing Black Cochins, White-crested Polish, and Rhode Island Reds were called "stiffeners," which were used to give support to cigarette packaging. The card with the Houdan is just an extra incentive to purchase a certain brand.

Cover Chicks

Abstract chickens

Edward Penfield (1866–1925) was an illustrious illustrator, art editor, and poster artist. He is credited with bringing an abstract quality to commercial art with his bold and simplified shapes, as exemplified by this beautiful Harper's *cover.*

Cute chicken

Jessie Willcox Smith was one of America's premier female illustrators. From 1917 to 1933, her art was featured on the cover of Good Housekeeping, *one of America's most popular magazines at that time.*

To the glory of France

This Vogue *cover was designed by noted artist Helen Dryden in 1918. Her statement about World War I exudes confidence and optimism, although the war would not be over for another six months. In her illustration, Dryden depicts a radiant, defiant woman poised triumphantly while holding a cockaded tricorn hat with a cock—the symbol of a free France—positioned regally.*

The Culinary Chicken

In addition to acquiring chickenalia, the easiest way to bring chickens into your daily life is via the kitchen. This tasty bird has probably inspired more imaginative cuisine than any other food product, with each dish reflecting the history of the country in which it is found. Economical and nutritious (that is, if you don't count the delicious, but fatty, skin), it is probably safe to say that chicken is the most universally eaten meat.

Although chicken is a staple of many diets around the world, its original function was not as a food. As mentioned, chickens were originally domesticated not for the delectability of their flesh, but for sport and for their eggs.

Although the chicken was an important part of ancient Greek culture and most Athenians owned a hen for egg laying, Greek cuisine was quite bland. The Greek diet consisted mostly of barley, olives, figs, and some goat's milk cheese. With limited ingredients, chicken meat was not a gourmet delight, and its consumption was mostly for religious purposes.

It was during the Roman Empire that chicken became a vital part of the daily diet. The toga-clad Romans made many advances in the culinary arts, including the creation of the capon. This was a period of much excess and moral laxity, including gluttonous and lavish feasts. In 161 B.C., the Senators, including the consul Caius Fannius, took legal action to curtail the extravagance that was rampant throughout the country. The Lex Fannia were established, restricting the cost of feasts and the number of guests and specifically forbidding the serving of any fowl except a hen, further adding that the hen could not be fattened.

To evade these laws, attention was turned to the rooster and how to make him fat and tender. It was discovered that by castrating a rooster (removing his testicles) he would grow plump and tasty. Voilà, the capon was created. Pliny the Elder noted that to fatten a cock quickly, one should place him in a cage so small he was unable to move, with nothing to do but eat. Varro added that hens could be fattened by feeding them such "goodies" as lizard fat and wheat bread soaked in wine, and they would "grow fat and tender in twenty days."

Some of the Roman methods of prepping the birds were quite unique. These practices included dipping a tough live hen in Falernian wine (a heavy, sweet red wine made from Falernian grapes and popular in ancient Rome) and water. Ulisse Aldrovandi claimed that meat could be tenderized by placing a fig in the creature's anus while it was still alive.

Every part of the chicken was used in ancient kitchens—the blood, intestines, testicles, rumps, livers, lungs, feet, heads, and necks. Crests and wattles were eaten in broth or roasted over coals with pepper and orange juice. Chicken brains were a delicacy, because they were said to heighten intelligence. Chicken livers were second in popularity only to those of geese. It was claimed that chicken livers roasted on coals quickly revived sagging strength, especially when accompanied by a little white wine.

Apicus, a Roman gourmet who lived in the first century A.D., is credited with writing the first cookbook in the Western world, one that included chicken recipes.

Pliny the Elder noted that some Roman diners reached such a degree of gluttonous pleasure that they ate only one part of the tender chicken and wasted the rest.

Gourmet-poet Yuan Mei (1716–1798) listed the chicken as one of "the four heroes of the table" in his *Sui Yuan Cookery Book* (the other heroes being pork, fish, and duck).

Chicken Marengo

1 (2–3 pound) chicken, cut up
¼ cup (½ stick) butter
2 medium onions
1 cup chicken stock
1 cup dry white wine
4 large tomatoes, peeled, seeded, and chopped
3 cloves garlic, sliced
1 teaspoon thyme
1 bay leaf
salt and pepper to taste
15–18 crayfish or medium-sized shrimp
12–16 medium-sized mushrooms
parsley for garnish

Brown chicken in butter for about 15 minutes. Remove and pour off all but 2 to 3 tablespoons of the butter. In the leftover butter, sauté the onions until golden. Add chicken, stock, wine, tomato, garlic, thyme, bay leaf, salt, and pepper. Bring to a boil, reduce heat and cover for 40 minutes or until chicken is tender. Add shellfish. Cook for eight minutes if shellfish is raw, two to three minutes if it has already been cooked.

Remove chicken and shellfish. Cook mushrooms in pan juices for 15 minutes. Pour juices over chicken and shellfish. Remove bay leaf and sprinkle with parsley before serving.

"Poultry is for the cook what canvas is for the painter."
— Jean Anthelme Brillat-Savarin (1755–1826), *Physiologie du Gout*

Here is one of many recipes attributed to Apicus: "Take a chicken, bone it, cut it up into small pieces and add chopped onion, coriander, skinned brains. Cook in liquamen [fish oil], oil and wine. When it is cooked, chop an onion and the coriander finely and strain over this the cooked peas, not yet seasoned. Take a suitable saucepan and arrange the ingredients all mixed together. Then crush pepper, cumin and add some chicken stock. Likewise, break in a mortar two eggs and mix with the other ingredients. Pour the remaining stock from the chicken over whole boiled peas and garnish with these or pine kernels. Cook over a low fire and serve."

In ancient Egypt, plump figures were in vogue for women, and chickens aided in the plumping process. Patrician Egyptian women bathed in the broth of plump black hens that had been fattened with hazelnuts, sweet almonds, pistachios, pine nuts, and peas. The women then ate the entire bird while in the bath. The lady of the house did this for a number of days to ensure chunking up.

Poultry has been prized in China for nearly 3,000 years. The rooster was believed to possess the yang or cosmic force of the masculine spirit. This appreciation of chicken naturally extended to food. Guided by the standards of Confucius more than 2,500 years ago, chefs took their delicate art to a higher level. His philosophy of harmony, beauty, and balance extended to the preparation and enjoyment of food. Confucius stressed that food should be considered more than life-sustaining—taste, color, texture, aroma, and presentation should come together in perfect harmony. Chicken was a high point of cuisine, reserved for special occasions. There were hundreds of chicken dishes, which Confucius empowered by giving them poetic names such as "Drunken Chicken" and "Chicken with Golden Pastures."

Since the early Middle Ages, chickens have been important in Jewish cooking. People were allowed to slaughter the chickens themselves, according to kosher laws. Raising poultry was a traditional occupation in Germany and Eastern Europe, where many Jews lived. In the Jewish tradition, chicken is a standard fare in such social affairs as weddings and bar mitzvahs. The classic Friday night family meal includes chicken soup, followed by roasted or boiled chicken.

What would the world be without Grandma's chicken soup when you have a cold? A twelfth-century Jewish physician,

Moses Maimonides, first suggested this cure. Since that time, scientists have acknowledged that chicken soup does have medicinal qualities to combat the common cold. Though how it does this is not totally understood, the soup seems to contain a beneficial substance that assists in clearing the nasal passages of mucus containing viruses and bacteria.

Throughout history, the French have taken the art of gastronomy very seriously. Around the first century, cookbook writer Apicus and Roman cuisine exerted a strong influence on French cooking, especially among the upper classes. Then, due to a long period of invasions, hardship, and famine, gastronomical advances were delayed until peace in Europe was gradually restored—albeit temporarily—around the eighth century. Poultry and fish became more plentiful in kitchens as farmers and fishermen were able to ply their trades and sell their wares. Traders pushing to the outer reaches of the known world and crusaders returning from exotic locales brought new spices to Europe. Increased use of condiments and spices meant that recipes and cooking techniques could become more and more elaborate, both in taste and presentation. Fanciful feasts and elaborate banquets became the rage in France among the royalty, and the royal menus often included stuffed capons and other tasty *poulets.* In his 1598 coronation speech, Henry IV (1553–1610) said, "I want there to be no peasant in my kingdom so poor that he is unable to have a chicken in his pot on Sundays." The famous *poule au pot,* a stuffed hen simmered with meat and vegetables, became a symbol of modest comfort for all French classes.

A well-known French recipe is Chicken Marengo, which was created by Chef Dunand for Napoleon I after the latter's narrow victory over the Austrians at the battle of Marengo in northern Italy. After the battle, a tired and hungry Napoleon returned to his tent. According to legend, his chef put a few chickens inthe frying pan, added a couple of tomatoes, some onions, and a few crayfish, and—*voilà!*—a new dish was born. Dunand started by deep frying the meat and the crayfish in hot oil. Cooking meat in oil makes the dish very heavy. In later modifications of the recipe, the chicken was only rapidly browned in oil and moistened with a little wine before the final frying. Henri Paul Pellaprat, a noted twentieth-century French chef, improved the dish by adding bouillon at the same time as the wine to moisten the meat. At first a fried dish, Chicken Marengo evolved into a stew.

Andre Dumas, author of the *Grand Dictionnaire de Cuisine,* published in 1873, wrote of a sure-fire method of fattening poultry in three weeks to a month. To produce the best possible taste and at the same time the greatest quantity of fat, one must "Feed them for a few days with ground barley, bran and milk. Put them in a cage in a dark place, but one which is not damp. Finally always leave within easy reach of them some barley that has been kneaded with milk." Dumas also recommended buckwheat for fattening farmyard birds destined for the gourmet's table.

Through my own gastronomic expeditions in France, I know that the Poulet de Bresse breed of chicken is among the most delicious fowl on the planet, due to a combination of genetics, diet, careful breeding, and strict selection. With this combination, these prized free-range, corn-and-milk-fed chickens and capons reach culinary

Broilers are small chickens weighing from one to two and one-half pounds.
Fryers weigh about three pounds.
Roasters weigh three and one-half pounds or more.

Chicken casserole

This piece was made in the United States by the Hull company. The company formed in Crooksville, Ohio, in 1905 closed in 1986. (Photograph by Michael Cleary)

Chicken Kiev

4 whole fresh chicken breasts (½ to ¾ pound each)
¾ cup (1½ sticks) unsalted butter, softened
2 eggs, beaten
2 cups bread crumbs
vegetable oil
salt and pepper

Between two sheets of wax paper, pound chicken breasts to ⅛ inch thick.

Make ½-inch-thick and 3-inch-long cylinder shapes out of butter. (If you want the butter to be a little tastier, add 1 teaspoon lemon juice, 1 teaspoon tarragon or chives, 1 tablespoon parsley, 2 tablespoons salt, and a little pepper to the butter.)

Assemble cutlets by wrapping chicken around the butter. Dip cutlets into beaten egg and then roll in bread crumbs. Refrigerate for two hours. Fry cutlets for about 5 minutes in 3–4 inches of oil that is 360 degrees. Keep warm in 200-degree oven for no more than 10 minutes until ready to serve.

perfection when prepared by a skilled chef. One of author Ernest Hemmingway's favorite dishes was Poulet de Bresse, and his favorite recipe included truffles and pâté de foie gras.

In 1607, chickens survived the perilous ninety-day trans-Atlantic crossing and arrived in Jamestown with the first settlers. *The First American Cookbook*, written in 1796 by Amelia Simmons, included a chicken recipe:

> Pick and clean six chickens, without scalding take out their inwards and wash the birds while whole, then joint the birds, salt and pepper the pieces and inwards. Roll one inch thick paste No. 8 and cover a deep dish, and double at the rim or edge of the dish, put thereto a layer of chickens and a layer of thin slices of butter, till the chickens and one and a half pound butter are expended, which cover with a thick paste: bake one and a half hour.
>
> Or if you be poor, parboil the chickens with half a pound of butter, and put the pieces with the remaining one pound of butter, and half the gravy into the paste, and while boiling, thicken the residue of the gravy and when the pie is drawn, open the crust and add the gravy.

Brunswick County, Virginia, lays claim to the original Brunswick stew. It was created for Dr. Creed Haskins, a member of the Virginia legislature, and his friends on a hunting trip by Dr. Haskins's cook "Uncle" Jimmy Matthews. The stew made its public debut at a political rally at the home of Dr. Haskins for Democratic presidential candidate Andrew Jackson in 1828. The dish was a smashing success, and all the guests were eager to go home and duplicate it. Soon variations started appearing throughout the South at political rallies, church suppers, and family reunions. Originally, the recipe featured squirrel, but chicken soon became the favored meat.

Speaking of Southern hospitality, no self-respecting Dixie dinner is complete without fried chicken. This popular dish originated in the antebellum South and was a highlight of lavish plantation banquets. Though recipes varied, all were complete with creamy gravy made from the drippings of the chicken, which had been fried in oil or bacon grease. After the opulent days of early plantation life, fried chicken continued to be a popular choice in every walk of life. At gatherings from church suppers to family reunions, the dish particularly became a staple of African-American cuisine.

There are a few theories on the origin of the well-known dish Chicken a la King. Many culinary historians credit Delmonico's, a noted restaurant in New York, with developing the dish. The restaurant named it after Foxhall Keene, the son of a successful Wall Street speculator, who allegedly suggested a pimento-laden cream sauce to the Delmonico chef. "Chicken a la Keene" later evolved into the more regal title of "Chicken a la King." This dish was popular during the Depression, a time when politicians were promising a chicken in every pot.

Chicken Tetrazzini is a chicken and pasta combination, complemented by mushrooms, almonds, and a sherry-and-cheese cream sauce. The dish commemorates Luisa Tetrazzini (1874–1940), a well-fed coloratura soprano, and was extremely popular around the beginning of the twentieth century.

Kotlety po-Kyivskomu, better known as Chicken Kiev, is a great Ukrainian dish made of deep-fried chicken cutlets wrapped around butter. The thought of its fat content makes coronary-conscious dieters grasp their hearts. But despite Chicken Kiev's richness, it remains a classic.

Monica Sheridan, in her book *The Art of Irish Cooking* (1996), described what might be one of the world's most unusual cooking styles in her "Tinkers' Chicken" recipe. Tinkers, or Travelers, as they are now known in Ireland, scorned rootedness and chose a life on the road. They were reputed to enjoy eating any free-range, but foolish, chicken that may wander near their caravans. To disguise the bird's misfortune, the Travelers devised an ingenious way of cooking the poor fowl:

1. Wring its neck and kill it
2. Do not pluck or gut the chicken
3. Encase the chicken in a plaster of soft mud
4. Dig a hole a foot deep and place the chicken inside, fill in with dirt and light a fire on top.
5. After three or four hours, when the fire has died down, dig up the chicken
6. Crack the casement, the feathers stick to the clay, and the chicken should be perfectly cooked!

Knowing my love of chickens, people often ask if I eat chickens. The answer is yes, although I have never eaten a chicken I liked personally. I have eaten a few Lakenvelder roosters that I once owned, because they were so mean and disruptive in the hen house. I called upon a friend to be their executioner. Now my husband does the requisite duty if we want a chicken for the Sunday pot. We also use a professional butcher when we have large numbers destined for sale.

"Take a faire chek, and skald him, and breke the skyn (as sone as he is scalded) in the necke behinde, and blowe him, and cast him in faire water and wassh him: and pen kette of pe hede and nek, and lete pe ffete be on al hole, and dreaw him clene: and pen pike faire parcelly, and parboile hit; And pen take hard yolkes of eyron, and hewe hem and pe parcelly togidre, and fressh grece, and caste there-to-pouder of ginger, peter a litel saffron and salt, And put al in-to-pe Chike, and put him on a Spitte; And thenne late him roste, and serue forth."

—*The Good Huswives Handmaid for Cookerie in Her Kitchin* (1597)

Our everyday china

This Poppy Trail place setting often graces our dining room table. Made by the Metlox Manufacturing Company in California, the Poppy Trail line was introduced in 1934. (Photograph by Michael Cleary)

Chapter 6

A Chicken Dictionary and Other Chicken Tidbits

No other animal has inspired the English language as much as the colorful, all-purpose chicken. The following "Chicken Dictionary" comprises only a few of the hundreds of chicken-related words and terms. Many scientific references, horticultural words relating to chickens, and obsolete words—most of them popular in England in the nineteenth century—didn't make the cut. What is disheartening about the Chicken Dictionary, however, is that not one of the chicken terms is complimentary!

Facing page:
Who needs cats and dogs?
An Indiana woman has decided that Silkie chickens make much better pets. (Photograph © J. C. Allen & Son, Inc.)

Inset:
ABC chicken plate
Alphabet plates such as this one served as a tool for teaching children the alphabet. They were most popular between 1780 and 1860, but are still being made today. (Photograph by Michael Cleary)

A bold statement

Products with the "Cocksure" label promulgated a message with complete confidence.

A Chicken Dictionary

alectryon: the Greek word for cock

In myth, Alectryon was asked by Ares to guard the door during the latter's tryst with Aphrodite in her husband's absence. Unfortunately, Alectryon fell asleep and was punished by being transformed into a cock, whose lot in life is to arouse the sleeping.

bantam (banty): a small version of large fowl; small person who is fond of fighting

bantam weight: a boxer weighing less than 118 pounds

biddy: a chicken (young or old) or a woman (old and gossipy)

capon: a castrated rooster, often fattened for eating; an effeminate man

I was always told that capons were castrated roosters. When I realized that cocks had no external testicles, I was very confused. Then I was informed that the testicles are located within the body. To castrate a cock, a small incision is made under the wing between the last two ribs, and the testicles, attached to the spinal column at the rear of the lungs, are removed.

Chanticleer, also Chantecler: a loud crower; a cock immortalized by Chaucer

chick: a young chicken; a young person; a young woman (slang)

chicken: a fowl of any age or sex; the flesh of a fowl; a child or inexperienced person; a loose woman; a coward; a homosexual; originally the plural of *chick*

Ancient Britons called them *cicen* and *ciceu,* perhaps trying to imitate the "cheep cheep" sound the birds made. Around 1300, the word had become *chikenes,* as noted in the writings of Chaucer. By the late 1500s, Shakespeare spells the word *chickens,* and in the King James Version of the Bible (1611) the word is spelled the same way (see Matthew 23:37, "Even as a hen gathereth

her chickens under her wings").
chicken colonel: a full colonel, as opposed to a lieutenant colonel, referring to the eagle on the shoulder of the colonel's uniform
chicken feed, also chicken money: small change
chicken-hearted, also chicken-livered, chicken-spirited: cowardly
chicken-pecked: similar to henpecked but by an aggressive child
chicken-pull: a contest of pulling apart a chicken clavicle to see who gets the longer part, the winner theoretically receiving the fulfillment of wishes
chicken scratch, also hen scratch, chicken tracks, hen tracks: illegible writing, often by doctors
chicken sexers: a gifted individual who has the uncanny ability to determine the sex of a chick shortly after it has hatched
chicken-toed: similar to pigeon-toed, having toes that turn in
cock: the adult male of the domestic fowl; a faucet or valve; a victor, one occupying a position of success and control; in firearms, the hammer on a gun; a penis, usually considered a vulgar term (in the southern part of the United States, *cock* refers to the genitalia of both the male and the female); nonsense, poppycock; or turf; turning upward, on a slant; small boat
-cock (suffix): decedent of, e.g. Hancock
cock-and-bull story: a rambling and fanciful tale

The term *cock-and-bull story* is derived from a mythical encounter in which a cock kills a bull.

cock and hen: including both men and women, often used to describe a party with both sexes
cockerel: a young, male domestic fowl
cock of the walk: an overbearing leader; also a famous trademark of the Marley Tile Company, which showed a strutting cock with the words "Cock-o'-the-Walk"
cock penny: a school fee
cockade: a rosette or knot of ribbon worn on a hat
cock-a-doodle-doo: a cock's crow at dawn
cock-a-hoop: boastful and boisterous speech; lively, in buoyant spirits
cock-a-leekie: a Scottish soup made from leeks, chicken broth, and cream, sometimes with prunes added

According to Scottish tradition, the loser of a cockfight became the base of the soup.

cockalorum: a little cock; a self-important man
cockapert: impudent
cock a snook: to thumb one's nose at someone
cock-brained: foolish or scatterbrained
cockcrow: the early morning crow by cock; dawn
cockatrice, also basilisk: a serpent-monster hatched from a rooster's egg that can kill with its glance or its incredibly bad breath; a pernicious person
cocked: having landed unevenly after a throw so that it is difficult to tell which face is up, as in dice; drunk
cockloft: an attic
cockney: a resident of the East End of London; the dialect or accent of an East Ender

Cockney originally referred to a "cock's egg," or one without a yoke. The word then became associated with a spoiled and often effeminate young man. Later and gradually, it was applied to the youth from the area of Cockney in London.

cockpit: in an airplane, the space set apart for the pilots; the driver's compartment of a race car; an area for cockfights; a place where many small battles take place; part of

To "get a lucky break" initially referred to the person winning the larger half of a wishbone contest.

"A chicken with its head cut off" is often used to describe a person who is frantically attempting to do too much. It is also a scientific phenomenon; after the poor thing has been decapitated, the chicken has the ability to run around for several minutes, and, interestingly enough, never bumps into anything.

To have "both the hen and the egg" means to have one's cake and eat it too.

"He came forth from an egg" describes a handsome person.

Cocktail Conversation

There are many differing opinions and no definitive explanation of the origin of the word *cocktail.* The following are various theories:

• An 1898 article in the *Culpepper Exponent,* a Virginia newspaper, says, "The cocktail was the invention of Col. Carter of Culpepper Court House, Va. Many years ago in that locality there was a wayside inn named 'The Cock and Bottle' the semblance of an old English tavern. It bore on its swinging sign the picture of a cock and bottle, meaning that draft and bottled ale could be had within—a 'cock' in the old vernacular meaning a tap. He who got the last and muddy portion of the tap was said to have received the 'cocktail.'"

• The word is derived from *cock-ale,* a drink popular in England in the seventeenth and eighteenth centuries. Supposedly, an old mashed up rooster was added to ten gallons of ale, along with a sack with raisins, mace, and cloves. The mixture was allowed to infuse for a week or so, then bottled and enjoyed.

• It came from the practice of toasting the victor of a cockfight. The number of feathers left in the cock's tail would be placed in the drink.

• It is derived from the French word *coquetier,* or egg cup. Around 1875, Antoine Amédée Peychaud, an apothecary from Santo Domingo, held social gatherings and served liquor concoctions in an egg cup. Supposedly, English-speaking guests would call the drink a *cocktay,* which eventually became the *cocktail.*

• The term is a corruption of *cock-ale,* a special part of the fighting cock's diet. If the ale was good for the cock, it was also good for the cocker.

• The drink was so named because it resembles the beautiful feathers in a cock's tail.

• *Cocktail* comes from the saying that a drink will "cock your tail."

• It comes from *cocktailings,* the word for the dregs of various casks that would be drained out of the cocks, or valves, mixed together, and sold as a cheap drink.

In English literature, Thomas Hughes (1822–1896, *Tom Brown's School Years*) and William Makepeace Thackeray (1811–1863, *The Newcomes*) both mention *cocktail* as a mixed drink.

a warship used as quarters or to house those wounded in battle; on a small decked vessel, the area toward the stern and lower than the rest of the deck, from which the vessel is steered.

Originally, cockpit applied only to the cockfighting ring. In 1599, Shakespeare used the term in *Henry V* to refer generally to the theater and specifically to the area around the stage. Beginning around 1700, the word was used as a nautical term to refer to the compartment below the decks of a warship, used for either sleeping quarters or a hospital. During World War I, fighter pilots began to call the pilot's cramped quarters a cockpit. In the mid 1930s, it was used to describe a part of the car.

cockscomb: the fleshy red crest on a rooster's head

cock's egg: a small yokeless egg

cockspur: the spur on the cock's leg

cock-stand: an erection (most often used in erotic Victorian literature)

cockstride: a short distance

cocksure: with complete security and certainty—often too much

cock-tease: a woman who uses her charms to stir lust in a gentleman's loins, only to then deny him "the goods"

To my knowledge, there is no male equivalent for this term.

cock-throwing: an old sport of throwing sticks at a cock tied to a stake

cock-up: a goof up

cocky: conceited, impudent

cold-cocked: to be knocked senseless

coquette: a female cock, a flirt

coxcomb: a foolish and vain man who is falsely proud of his achievements

dunghill fowl: a common domestic fowl, a chicken "mutt"

fowl: a bird of any kind, including guinea

fowl and peacocks, as well as chickens
Gallus: the Latin word for cock
Gallus domesticus: the scientific name of the chicken
Gallus gallus: scientific name for the Red Jungle Fowl, the domestic chicken's evolutionary ancestor
hen: a mature female of common domestic fowl
hen coop: a women's college dorm
hen house: an army officer's club; a house controlled by a woman
henhussy: a man who takes too much interest in women's affairs
hen party: a party for women only
henpecked: dominated by a nagging, annoying wife, as in "a henpecked husband"

This expression became popular in the late seventeenth century, when Lord Byron wrote in his poem *Don Juan*, "Oh! ye lords of ladies intellectual, inform us truly, have they not henpecked you all?"

hen-pen: a girl's school
hensure: overly self-confident, said of women
hen wife: a woman who raises poultry
pecking order: a social hierarchy of dominance and subordination

The identification of a pecking order is attributed to Norwegian psychologist T. Schjelderup-Ebbe, who noted that in a flock of hens, there is a descending order of dominating hens, from the top hen who pecks on all the others down to the last who is pecked on by all. A hen may change her position in the hierarchy by winning a fight with a superior hen. The pecking order becomes much more complex when roosters are added to the equation, as dominating hens may repel the advancements of lesser males. I have witnessed many a poor hen at the bottom of the pecking order. In my own flock, Betty, a Polish hen with a gorgeous set of head feathers, was plucked bald by jealous, old, matronly hens. This order of social dominance and subordination is found in most animal communities, including those of humans.

pecker: a nose or beak; courage or pluck; a penis

In England, "Keep your pecker up" means keep your spirits or courage up. Anatomically, the word refers to a beak or nose. However, a pecker in the United States refers to a different anatomical part than in England, and telling Americans to keep their pecker up would cause a snicker.

peckish: irritable, hungry
poultry: domesticated birds that serve as a source for meat and eggs; refers to chickens as well as other fowl—ducks, turkeys, and geese
pullets: young female chickens who have not begun to lay eggs
roost: to sit on a perch; to lodge for a night
rooster: an adult male domesticated fowl
rooster tail: a high-arching spray of water thrown up behind a fast-moving motorboat
spring chicken: literally, a chicken born in the spring; figuratively, a young person

Before the onset of incubators and warming houses, farmers found that chicks born in the early spring brought the best prices. Wise buyers would know the difference between a plump and tender bird—a spring chicken—and a tough old hen—not

Freak chicken

Burdette E. Cowles, from Forestville, Connecticut, holds his four-legged chicken in this photo from the early 1900s. He claimed the extra appendages caused a swelling in the cranium, and the cocky rooster strutted around all day, tiring less quickly than his two-legged friends.

An early cock reference

This detail from a 1497 illustration by Albrecht Dürer illustrates the connection between the terms stopcock *(a spigot) and* cock*, and their anatomical allusions. Notice the man on the left, leaning on the post. That spigot with the rooster on top is certainly placed in a strategic spot.*

a spring chicken. Hence the derogatory expression, "She's no spring chicken."

white feather: a sign used to designate a coward

This term originated in cockfighting days and indicated a crossbreed of cock (only cocks with red and black feathers were said to be of pure stock). "To show the white feather" implies a display of impure strain as well as cowardice. During World War I, men who did not fight were stigmatized with a white feather.

How the Rooster Became the Cock

The word *cock* as an anatomical description is often thought to derive from *stopcock*, which is a cylindrically shaped spigot that spews liquid. My guess is that the anatomical likeness of the rooster's head and neck to the male sexual organ began this age-old association.

In the Middle Ages the words *cock* and *prick* became acceptable substitutes for the word *penis*. In the *Oxford Dictionary* (1618), the cock appears innocently symbolic: "Whether referring to the whole man or to his instrument of procreation, the bird is one of the principle symbols of masculinity, along with the bull."

Until about 1830, the word *cock* was socially acceptable. However, with the onset of Victorian mores the word *cock* was deemed to be a vulgarity. (At that time, most likely any word that alluded to the male organ was indecent.) In fact, the word was considered so deplorable that Bronson Alcott, the father of *Little Women* author Louisa May Alcott, changed the spelling of the family name from Allcock.

In *Word Origins and Their Romantic Stories* (1950), etymologist Wilfred Funk says that the word *cock* stands for *rooster*, or merely a fellow who roosts. But he also says "the word 'cock' developed what we can call in a nice way figurative associations. When these became widely enough known among men and boys, the term grew indecent and unspeakable and remains in men's language only. . . . [I]t is now on its way out and is only used by literati or by naive maiden aunts for both the fowl and the water faucet!" The anatomical implication of the word *cock* still persists today, and many still snicker at the word. The word *cockerel* was often used instead of *cock* to describe the rooster.

The Chicken Facts of Life

This may come as a shock to those who aren't chicken aficionados, and my intent is not to embarrass or malign the rooster, but—in basic terms—the cock has no cock. Instead, both he and the hen each have a single orifice called a cloaca (stemming from the French word for sewer), which serves a multitude of functions, including reproduction.

Chicken sex is rather comical. The rooster seems to perform his duty swiftly, violently, and seemingly without emotion. (The lack of emotion is perhaps due to the fact that it is the rooster's job to service a multitude of hens a day.) He pounces on the hen's back, often grabbing the back of her neck with his beak, gyrates a bit, and sprays his "magic dust." The hen then wiggles until the dust transfers into her cloaca from his. This entire process, called the "Cloacal Kiss," takes a few seconds.

The Chicken of Your Dreams

Speaking of cloacas, Sigmund Freud, the founder of psychoanalysis, espoused "the cloaca theory." In essence, the theory says that in childhood, the female orifices are perceived as a single opening. It is later, according to Freud, that one discovers that there are actually two cavities. This theory is illustrated in dreams, such as one in which a familiar house with one room is divided into two or vice versa.

It is not surprising that with the amount of time I spend thinking about chickens, chickens would spill over into my REM state. I dream about chickens often, though seemingly not in a profound, symbolic way. My chicken dreams relate to finding chickens in odd places. Perhaps this is a Freudian wish dream, relating to my obsession with finding chickens in art, culture, music, fables, and many other things.

Other chicken dreams are said to have specific meanings. For example, it is said that if you dream that chickens are entering your house, you will be enriched with wealth and honor. If you turn into a chicken in your dream, your unconscious believes that you are turning into a coward. If you dream about roosters, there is lust in your loins.

Some have thought dreams of chickens were bad omens. For instance, dreaming of a crowing capon meant sadness and trouble. Other dreams of chickens predicted bad luck. If the chickens in the dream were roosting, the trouble would manifest itself in domestic affairs and would be rather insignificant. If the rooster in the dream was strutting, the bad luck would be more severe and would extend to business. It is said that if you dream of a hen and chicks, your

Eggs purchased in the store are not fertilized; hence it is not necessary for a chicken to engage in "chicken sex" to create an egg.

"Curses are like young chickens, they always come home to roost."
—Robert Southey (1774–1843), *The Curse of Kehama*

How to Say "Cock-a-doodle-doo" in Twenty-one Different Languages

Chinese: *gue-gue ou gou-gou*
Danish: *kykliky*
English: *cock-a-doodle-doo*
Finnish: *kukkokeikuu*
French: *cocorico*
German: *kikeriki*
Greek: *kikiriki*
Hebrew: *coucouricou*
Gaelic: *cuc-a-dudal-du*
Italian: *chicchirichi*
Japanese: *kou-kou-kou-kou*
Dutch: *kukeluki*
Norwegian: *kukkeliky*
Polish: *kukuryky*
Portuguese: *cocorococo*
Romanian: *cucurigu*
Russian: *kou-ka-re-kou*
Serbo-Croatian: *kukuriky*
Spanish: *quiquiriqui*
Swedish: *kuckeliku*

PORTRAIT OF THE "COCHIN-CHINA" FOWL!

Right and facing page:
Cochin comparison
A cartoon from George P. Burnham's The History of the Hen Fever *(1855, see chapter 1) illustrates just how big the country's Cochin craze was. However, Burnham's tall, thin birds looked little like today's full-figured and full-feathered Cochins. (Photograph © Lynn M. Stone)*

lover will betray you and marry another. Farmers who dream of chickens will have a bad crop and will lose many chickens. Businessmen who dream of chickens can expect to be defrauded by a con artist, and sailors can fear losing their goods or narrowly escaping a shipwreck.

Chicken Superstitions

There are hundreds of superstitions involving chickens, many on the subject of romance and marriage.

In Thuringia, Germany, and Silesia, Poland, girls who wanted to marry would knock three times against the wall of the chicken coop. If a rooster crowed, they would marry the next year. If a hen clucked, they would have a long wait until the altar.

In nineteenth-century England, a young woman would look through a keyhole on Saint Valentine's morning. If she saw a cock and hen, her wedding would occur before the end of the year.

Superstitions from other parts of the world say:

- If a girl wanted to dream of her future husband, she would put an egg under her pillow.
- If you ate five gizzards in one day, you could marry anyone you like.
- If you ate an eggshell full of salt before going to bed then dreamt that someone brought you water, that someone will be your future spouse.
- If you put a wishbone above your door, the first person to enter would be the one you would marry, and the marriage would take place within ten days.
- If a hen laid two eggs in one day, it was a sign that kinfolk will marry.

Appendix

Table of Breeds

This table of breeds was compiled from many sources. It cannot boast to be the definitive or complete list. In fact, I am not certain if one exists. But it demonstrates that the list of chicken breeds goes on and on and on.

I have listed the breeds by their country of origin, although in some instances where they hailed from is unclear. Those breeds with an asterisk (*) presently belong to the *American Standard of Perfection*.

Australia
Australorp*
Australian (Chinese) Langshan
Australian Game
Australian Pit Game

Austria
Altsteirer
Sulmtaler

Belgium
Antwerp Belgium (a.k.a. Belgium Bearded d'Anvers; bantam only)*
Belgian Bearded d'Uccle (bantam only)
Belgian Game
Brabanconne
Campine (a.k.a. Braekel)*
Eikenberger
Grubbe Bearded Bantam
Herve
Mechelner
Mille Fleure, sometimes referred to as Millie
Tournai Bantam (a.k.a. Flanders)
Uckle Bearded Bantam
Watermaal Bearded Bantam

Brazil
Musician Fowl

Bulgaria
Shumen Black
Stara Zagora Red

Canada
Chantecler*

Chile
Araucana*

China
Black Jiuyan
Brahma*
Chabo Bantam (developed in Japan)
Chahua
Chinese Game
Cochin*
Jingyuan
Langshan*
Lindian
Malay*
Nankin (bantam only)
New Yangzhou
Pekin (bantam only)
Putong
Silkie*
Silkie Taihe
Wuding

Cuba
Cubalaya*

Czechoslovakia
Bohemian Fowl

Denmark
Danish Land Hen

Egypt
Fayoumi

Finland
Finnish Home Breed Chicken

France
L'Alsacienne
Bassette
Bresse-Gauloise
La Charollaise
Le Combattant du Nord
Crevecoeur*
Faverolle*
La Fleche*
Gatinaise
Houdan*
La Lyonnaise
Marans
Meusienne
Pictave
Poulet de Bresse

Germany
Augsburger
Bergische Kraher
Bielefelder Kennhuhner
Booted Bantams
Dresdener
Kruper
Niederrheiner
Ostriesische Mowen
Rhinelander
Sulmater
Thuringian Bearded Fowl
Vorwerk Huhner
Westfalische Totleger

Hungary
Brahma
Kadakanath
Magyar Chicken
Naked Neck* (a.k.a. Transylvanian Naked Neck or Turken)

India
Aseel*
Brahma*
Jungle Fowl
Kadakanath

Indonesia
Sumatra*

Iran
Rumpless Fowl

Italy
Ancona*
Leghorn*
Polish (a.k.a. Polands or Paduans)*

Japan
Frizzle★
Japanese★ (bantam only)
Phoenix★
Shamo★
Tosa Onagadori
Yokohama★
Tomaru
Yamato Gunkei
Chibi Shamo
Ko Shamo

Malasia
Malay★
Serama (a.k.a. Sri Rama)

The Netherlands
Barnvelder★
Bearded Polish★
Breda
Dutch Bantam
Dutch Booted Bantam
Dutch Crested
Dutch Owlbeard
Drente
Freisian
Groninger Meeuwen
Grubbe Bearded Bantam
Hamburg★
Kraaikop
Lakenvelder★
Netherlands Krulbaardkuifhoen
Noord-Hollandse Fowl
Old Dutch Bantam
Non Bearded Polish★
Sabelpoot Bantam
Twente Grey
Welsummer★

Norway
Jaer Fowl

Paraguay
Langosta

Poland
Greenleg Partridge
Polbar

Russia
Adler Silver
Orloff (originally from Persia)
Poltava Clay Colored
Ukraine Crested
Ukraine Ushanki
Yurlov Golosysti

Sicily
Sicilian Buttercup★

South Africa
Natal Game
Potchefstroom Koekoek

Spain
Andalusian★
Black Sumatra Game
Catalana★ (a.k.a. Prat or Caraland Del Prat Leonada)
Leon
Minorca★
Penedesenca
White Faced Black Spanish★

Sweden
Queen Silvia
Svart Höna (a.k.a. Swedish Black Hen)

Switzerland
Appenzeller Spitzhauben
Appenzeller Barthuhner

Turkey
Denizili
Sultan

United Kingdom
Cochin Bantam★
Cornish★
Dorkings★
Golden Duckwing
Modern Game Bantam★
Modern Game★
Old English Game★
Orpington★
Red Cap★
Rosecomb (bantam only)★
Sebright★ (bantam only)
Scots Dumpy (developed in Scotland)
Sultan★
Sussex★

United States
Ameraucana★
Buckeye★
Delaware★
Dominique★
Holland★
Plymouth Rock★
Java (originally came from Java but was developed in the United States)★
Jersey Giant★
Lamona★
New Hampshire★
Rhode Island Red★
Rhode Island White★
Wyandotte★

Zimbabwe
Shona Fowl

Of unknown origin
Pyncheon Bantam

Reading and References

Aldrovandi, Ulisse. *Aldrovandi on Chickens*. Translated by L. R. Lind. Norman: University of Oklahoma Press, 1963.

Alken, Henry. *The National Sports of Great Britain*. London: Methuen & Co., 1903.

American Standard of Perfection. American Poultry Association, 1998.

American Standard of Excellence as Revised by the United Poultry Fanciers of America. American Poultry Association, 1874.

Andersen, Hans Christian. *It's Perfectly True and Other Stories*. Translated by Paul Leyssac. New York: Harcourt, Brace & World, 1938.

Baring-Gould, William S., and Ceil Baring-Gould. *The Annotated Mother Goose, Nursery Rhymes Old and New*. New York: Bramhill House, 1962.

Batty, Joseph. *Lewis Wright's Poultry*. Hindhead, Surrey: Triplegate Ltd.; Liss, Hants, England: Distributed by Nimrod Book Services, 1983.

Bement, C. N. *American Poulterer's Companion*. New York: Harper & Brothers Publishers, 1867.

Black, Mary C., and Jean Lipman. *American Folk Painting*. New York: C.N. Potter, 1966.

Brillat-Savarin, Jean Anthelme. *The Physiology of Taste: Meditations on Transcendental Gastronomy*. New York: Liveright Publishing Corporation, 1948.

Brion, Marcel. *Animals in Art*. Translated by Frances Hogarth-Gaute. New York: Franklin Watts, 1959.

Cadbury, Warder H. *Arthur Fitzwilliam Tait, Artist in the Adirondacks*. Newark: University of Delaware Press; Cranbury, NJ: Associated University Presses, 1986.

Charbonneau-Lassay, Louis. *The Bestiary of Christ*. Translated by D. M. Dooling. New York: Parabola Books, 1991.

Clark, Joseph D. *Beastly Folklore*. Metuchen, N.J.: Scarecrow Press, 1968.

Clark, Willene B., and Meradith T. McMunn, eds. *Beasts and Birds of the Middle Ages: The Bestiary and Its Legacy*. Philadelphia: University of Pennsylvania Press, 1989.

Cooper, J. C. *An Illustrated Encyclopaedia of Traditional Symbols*. London: Thames & Hudson, 1978.

Cox, Neil, and Deborah Povey. *A Picasso Bestiary*. London: Academy Editions, 1995.

De Fouilloy, Hugh. *The Medieval Book of Birds Hugh of Fouilloy's Aviarium*. Edited and translated by Willene B. Clark. Binghamton, New York: Medieval & Renaissance Text & Studies, 1992.

De Jong, H. M. E. *Michael Maier's Atalanta Fugiens Sources of an Alchemical Book of Emblems*. Leiden, Netherlands: E.J. Brill, 1969.

Dennis, James M. *Grant Wood: A Study in American Art and Culture*. Columbia: University of Missouri Press, 1986.

Driskell, David C. *Two Centuries of Black American Art*. Los Angeles: Los Angeles County Museum of Art; New York: Random House, 1976.

Eisler, Colin. *Durer's Animals*. Washington: Smithsonian Institution Press, 1991.

Evans, Bergen. *Dictionary of Quotations*. New York: Delacorte Press, 1968.

Evans, E. P. *The Criminal Prosecution and Capital Punishment of Animals*. London: W. Heinemann, 1906.

Ezra, Kate. *Royal Art of Benin: The Perls Collection in the Metropolitan Museum of Art*. New York: The Metropolitan Art Museum; distributed by Harry N. Abrams, 1992.

Freidmann, Herbert. *A Bestiary for Saint Jerome: Animal Symbolism in European Religious Art*. Washington: Smithsonian Institution Press, 1980.

Garwood, Darrell. *Artist in Iowa: A Life of Grant Wood*. New York: W.W. Norton & Company, 1944.

George, M. Dorothy. *Hogarth to Cruikshank: Social Chance in Graphic Satire*. London: Viking Penguin Books Limited, 1967.

Goodrich, Lloyd. *Yasuo Kuniyoshi*. New York: Whitney Museum of American Art; Macmillan, 1948.

Grandville, J.J. *Bizarreries and Fantasies of Grandville: 266 illustrations from Un autre monde and Les animaux*. Edited by Stanley Appelbaum. New York: Dover Publications, 1974.

Grimm, Jacob, and Wilhelm Grimm. *Fairy Tales*. New York: McLoughlin Brothers's, n.d.

Hale, William Harlan and the editors of Horizon Magazine. *The Horizon Cookbook and Illustrated History of Eating and Drinking through the Ages*. New York: American Heritage Publishing, 1968.

Harris, Warren G. *Gable and Lombard.* New York: Simon and Schuster, 1974.

Hendricks, Gordon. *The Life and Works of Winslow Homer.* New York: Harry N. Abrams, 1979.

Hickman, Money L., and Yasuhiro Sato. *The Paintings of Jakuchu.* New York: Harry N. Abrams, 1989.

Hobbs, Robert. *Milton Avery.* New York: Hudson Hills Press, 1990.

Hopf, Alice L. *Chickens and Their Wild Relatives.* New York: Dodd, Mead & Company, 1982.

Huffington, Arianna Stassinopoulos. *Picasso: Creator and Destroyer.* New York: Simon and Schuster, 1988.

Ingersoll, Ernest. *Birds in Legend Fable and Folklore.* New York: Longmans, Green and Co., 1923.

James, Thomas. *Aesop's Fables: Chiefly from Original Sources.* New York: Grosset & Dunlap Publishers, n.d.

Jull, M. A. "The Races of Domestic Fowl," *National Geographic,* April 1927.

Klingender, Francis Donald. *Animals in Art and Thought to the End of the Middle Ages.* Cambridge, Mass.: M.I.T. Press, 1971.

La Fontaine, Jean de. *The Fables of Jean de la Fontaine.* Translated by Joseph Auslander and Jacques Le Clercq. New York: The Limited Editions Club, 1930.

———. *Selected Fables.* Translated by Eunice Clark. New York: Dover Publications, 1968.

Lehner, Ernst and Johanna. *A Fantastic Bestiary: Beasts and Monsters in Myth and Folklore.* New York: Tudor Publishing Company, 1969.

L'Ertrange, Sir Roger. *Fables of Aesop and other Eminent Mythologists: with Morals and Reflections.* London: Printed for R. Sare and Others, 1699.

Leach, Maria, ed. *Dictionary of Folklore Mythology and Legend.* New York: Funk & Wagnalls Company, 1972.

Lowry, Thea. *Empty Shells: The Story of Petaluma, America's Chicken City.* Novato, Calif.: Manifold Press, 2000.

Mandeville, Paul, ed. *Eggs.* Chicago: Progress Publications, 1933.

Maresca, Frank, and Roger Ricco. *American Self-Taught: Paintings and Drawings by Outsider Artists.* New York: Alfred A. Knopf, 1993.

Morgan, Harry T. *Chinese Symbols and Superstitions.* South Pasadena, Calif.: P. D. and Ione Perkins, 1942.

Murayama, Hashime. "Fowl of the Old and New World," *National Geographic,* April 1927.

Oliver, Raymond. *Gastronomy of France.* Translated by Claude Durrell. London: George Rainbird Limited, 1967.

Opie, Iona and Moira Tatem, eds. *A Dictionary of Superstitions.* Oxford [England]; New York: Oxford University Press, 1989.

Oster, Maggie, ed. *The Illustrated Bird.* Garden City, NY: Dolphin Books, 1978.

Panati, Charles. *Extraordinary Origins of Every Day Things.* New York: Harper & Row, 1987.

Parmelee, Alice. *All the Birds of the Bible: Their Stories, Identification and Meaning.* New York: Harper & Brothers, 1959.

Paulson, Ronald. *Hogarth: His Life, Art, and Times.* New Haven, Conn.: Yale University Press, 1971.

Reed, Henry M. *The A. B. Frost Book.* Rutland, Vt.: Charles E. Tuttle Company, 1967.

Roden, Claudia. *The Book of Jewish Food: An Odyssey from Samarkand to New York.* New York: Alfred A. Knopf, 1996.

Rosenberg, Jakob, Seymour Slive, and E. H. ter Kuile. *Dutch Art and Architecture: 1600 to 1800.* New York: Penguin Books, 1977.

Rowland, Beryl. *Birds with Human Souls: A Guide to Bird Symbolism.* Knoxville: University of Tennessee Press, 1978.

Sheridan, Monica. *The Art of Irish Cooking.* New York: Hippocrene Books, 1996.

Shipley, Joseph T. *Dictionary of Word Origins.* New York: The Philosophical Library, 1945.

Smith, Page, and Charles Daniel. *The Chicken Book.* Boston: Little Brown and Company, 1975.

Stromberg, Loyl. *Poultry of the World.* Port Perry, Ontario, Canada: Silvio Mattacchione & Company, 1996.

Todd Warner Studio, Inc., 155 NW Eleventh St., Boca Raton, FL, 33432, www.toddwarner-studio.com

Toulouse-Lautrec, Henri de. *Toulouse-Lautrec: His Complete Lithographs and Drypoints.* Edited by Jean Adhemar. New York: Harry N. Abrams, 1965.

Van Loon, Hendrik Willem. *The Arts.* New York: Simon and Schuster, 1937.

Walters, Derek. *Ming Shu: The Art and Practice of Chinese Astrology.* New York: Simon & Schuster, 1987.

Walther, Ingo F., and Rainer Metzger. *Marc Chagall, 1887–1985: Painting as Poetry.* Translated by Michael Hulse. Köln, Germany: Benedikt Taschen, 1993.

Waters, Clara Erskine Clement. *A Handbook of Christian Symbols and Stories of the Saints as Illustrated in Art.* Boston: Ticknor and Company, 1886.

Ward, Charles A. *Oracles of Nostradamus.* New York: Gordon Press, 1975.

Werner, Alfred. *Chiam Soutine.* New York: Harry N. Abrams, 1985.

Index

Photo by Martin Hintz

About the Author

Pam Percy has been raising chickens as a hobby since 1986 on her five-acre property in Milwaukee, Wisconsin. She has been an avid collector of chicken art and "chickenalia" for nearly as long. When she realized that literature on chickens in art and culture was very limited, she decided to write a book to fill the void. She quit her job as the managing director of a theater company in Milwaukee and spent a year visiting various libraries and museums—in Milwaukee, New York, Washington D.C., Chicago, and London—in search of "chicken enlightenment." The result is her first book, *The Complete Chicken*, and her website, www.thecompletechicken.com.

Pam is also the executive producer of *Hotel Milwaukee,* a comedy/variety program aired on Wisconsin Public Radio, and an independent special events coordinator. She lives with her husband, writer Martin Hintz.